FROM *I LOVE LUCY* TO *SHŌGUN* ... AND BEYOND

Tales from the Other Side of the Camera

JERRY LONDON
and
Rhonda Collier

JERRY LONDON

DEDICATION

To Marilynn, Lisa, and Todd—with love and gratitude

.

ACKNOWLEDGEMENTS

Very Special Thanks To:

My writing partner, **Rhonda Collier**, whose wit, artistry with words, and tireless efforts brought my stories to life and made this book a reality.

My editor, **Amy Hawes**, who put it all together. She has a great eye and ear for content and dialogue, always making the book better.

Michael Brown, my good friend, producing partner, and editor for thirty years.

Ed Feldman, producer of *Hogan's Heroes*, who believed in me and launched my career as a director.

Eric Bercovici, writer/producer of *Shōgun*—my best friend and ally who lived with me through the biggest Japanese adventure of all time.

Duke Vincent, Aaron Spelling's partner, who gave me free reign as a director to create new shows for The Spelling Company.

Tony Barr, who, as the Head of Current Programming at ABC, gave me my first dramatic assignment as a director.

Lisa London, my creative daughter who motivated me to write this book and worked tirelessly in the editing process.

Marilynn London, my wife, for living through my adventurous career, working on my productions, and handling everything from our home to our children when I was on the road.

HOLLYWOOD SPEAKS ON
FROM *I LOVE LUCY* TO *SHŌGUN* . . .
AND BEYOND

"Thanks to Director Jerry London, playing John Blackthorn in James Clavell's *Shōgun* was perhaps the high point in my long career. In his new book, *From I Love Lucy to Shōgun . . . and Beyond*, Jerry brings back a deluge of exciting memories of our six-and-a-half-month shoot in Japan, and what a magnificent time it was! Jerry not only created one of the finest shows ever to grace TV, he now writes about that fabulous experience with wit and charm."
Richard Chamberlain—*Star of* Shōgun

"Jerry London is a legend in our business. He writes the way he directs, with pace and energy, and tells a great story. Plus a large dollop of humor and a love for what he does and the people involved in our great profession. This is a glorious read!"
Liam Neeson—*Star of* Star Wars

"Brilliant! I couldn't put it down. Even after working on *Dr. Quinn, Medicine Woman* for six seasons with Jerry London, I am still surprised (and sometimes shocked) at all he has seen and been through in his long career. This book is for anyone who has ever wondered what goes on on a set when the cameras *aren't* rolling! A laugh-out-loud page turner."
Jane Seymour—*Star of* Dr. Quinn, Medicine Woman

"Jerry London, one of the most iconic directors and editors of television, has given us a book that will make you laugh and understand, and bring you insight into the art of storytelling through the medium that changed the world."
Edward James Olmos—*Actor/producer/director, star of* Blade Runner

"Jerry London was lucky enough to land in the middle of a great era of television history, and smart enough and talented enough to direct a huge chunk of it. His book takes the reader through that era at a gallop with refreshing wit and style. Nobody will put it down!"
Stuart Woods—*Best-selling author, writer of* Chiefs

"A master filmmaker shares his talented vision. . . . Now *that's* entertainment!"
Alfred R. Kelman—*Emmy Award-winning producer of* The Body Human

"A brilliant bio about a brilliant career! In my forty years as a producer/writer who worked with hundreds of directors, I never met one who surpassed Jerry's genius. Read his autobiography and you won't be confused about my reasons. Congrats on a job very, *very* well done!"
Duke Vincent—*Writer/producer, partner of Aaron Spelling Productions*

"Jerry London's book is a fascinating insider's look at some of our biggest TV shows and miniseries. From tips on directing to frank and funny stories about the Hollywood stars he's worked with, London takes us on an unforgettable journey through the Golden Age of Television."
James Conway—*Director/producer of* Charmed

"A great read! Fun, educational, inspiring. Didn't want it to end."
Linda Bergman—*Writer/producer of* The Barbara Mandrell Story

"Alive with the excitement of Hollywood and peppered with cinematic recollections by the award-winning director, Jerry London, as he reveals behind-the-camera events and untold stories of his directing adventures with famous stars, fabulous locations, and demanding producers in a whirlwind career, this book is a must read for all film buffs. Very highly recommended!"
Michael Brown—*Emmy Award-winning editor/author*

"Jerry London grew up on the same mean streets of Hollywood as me. So as one local director kid to another . . . man, your book is BRILLIANT! It's the most FUN and INSIGHTFUL look into our industry's formative decades that I've *ever* read. Jerry was at the helm of so many of television's greatest achievements. And, boy, does he have GREAT STORIES from the trenches! Do you love "addictive-can't-stop-reading" books? THIS IS IT!!!"

Tom McLoughlin—*Director/writer/producer,* Friday the 13th Jason Lives

"Hey Jer, I finished your book today. Nice job! I found it personal and fun to read. I actually finished it in two sittings. Your storytelling pulls us in and keeps us in. It will be hard for any future readers to put the book down. Congratulations!"

Granville Van Dusen—*Actor, star of* Gettysburg

"There are so many things I could say about director Jerry London. On Jerry's set, "acting" was not allowed. It was always about "being." One day as I was rehearsing an emotional scene in *The Ordeal of Bill Carney*, Jerry gently leaned in and privately whispered, "Don't 'do' anything. Just be." A director that has such a sense of truth is priceless to an actor. Thank you, Jerry."

Ana Alicia—*Actress, star of* Falcon Crest

"If you've been looking for a book on directing, look no further. Jerry London's prodigious career is excellently detailed in *From I Love Lucy to Shogun . . . and Beyond.* A thoroughly engaging memoir that delineates his work with hundreds of luminaries, performers, and talented behind-the-scenes artists. From his beginning work as an apprentice editor, to expertly helming both episodic dramas and comedies, to his masterful directing of long form television including *Chiefs, Wheels, Ellis Island,* and the incomparable *Shōgun,* this book is informative, illuminating, and, ultimately, inspirational."

Charles Floyd Johnson—*Emmy Award-winning producer,* NCIS

"This is truly an *insider's* view of show business from the most prolific television director of his time. Jerry—who is directly responsible for some of the most acclaimed movies and miniseries of all time—names the "names" and pulls no punches as he takes us behind the celebrity-packed scenes of Hollywood. More than just a series of reminiscences, Jerry delivers great insights and priceless advice for anyone hoping to build their

own show business career. I dare you to open it, because you won't put it down!"
Bob McCullough—*Supervising producer,* Falcon Crest

"Far back in the seventies or eighties, I can't remember which, my wife and I were huge fans of that exciting and superbly made television miniseries, *Shōgun*. It starred Richard Chamberlain, and was brilliantly and almost singlehandedly woven together by one Jerry London.

"Each episode raised the level of excellence to greater heights and revealed what courage and risk-taking imagination was essential to undertake this daunting task. It proved, without question, that Mr. London was and is an artist of the very first rank.

"What a thrill then, when sometime later Mr. London, taking a somewhat bolder risk, cast me to play opposite Gregory Peck and Sir John Gielgud in *The Scarlet and the Black.* Now, I had known both Greg Peck and Sir John already, but I'd never met Mr. London. I'd imagined a vastly experienced guru of substantial age, wise in years, severe in countenance, intolerant of fools, short in temper, and frighteningly awesome in power. How wrong could I have been?

"What I got instead was a charming, modest, enthusiastic young man, at least seventeen years my junior—almost a boy in fact—with a bounding energy and an outrageous sense of humor that bordered mercifully on the irreverent!

"Jerry turned out to be one of a handful of superheroes in my life who convinced me that hard work should have an abundance of joy in it or it isn't worth the candle.

"Now that I've been so nice to you, Jerry, for God's sake come back and direct me again. I'm massively available."
Christopher Plummer—*Academy Award-winning actor*

Table of Contents

JERRY LONDON

PREFACE

How did the scrawny kid standing in the middle of the tennis courts at Alhambra High School end up standing in the middle of the Roman Colosseum with Gregory Peck and Christopher Plummer? How did he go from looking through the lens of an old 35mm camera to looking out the window of Gina Lollobrigida's bedroom?

It was an exciting journey that led me to direct over three hundred fifty episodic television shows, forty Movies of the Week, and eleven miniseries, while working with over twenty-five Academy Award-winning actors and actresses.

"Director" means you are the problem solver. As Captain of the Ship, you must think on your feet and be able to turn on a dime, because you are who everyone is looking to for the final word . . . especially when things don't go quite as planned.

Having directed some of the greatest, funniest, most neurotic, generous, deranged, and brilliantly talented film and television stars of all time, the echo of "What Could Possibly Go Wrong?" followed me every step of the way.

There is no greater truth than this: Fact is far more interesting than fiction—and sometimes much harder to believe!

Come with me as I take you on a journey that is in essence a trip through the most dramatic growth in television's history, from the sets of some of TV's earliest shows and most outstanding dramas to Made for Television movies and miniseries. This is the story of how I went from an apprentice film editor to a sought-after director, embracing the challenges, the life-changing moments, and the grace of the people who believed in me along the way.

I hope that, perhaps in some small way, some of these tales will inspire you to be persistent and to keep your eye on the lens of the life you dream about.

DESILU TECH

I t was hot. Really hot. With record-breaking heat pushing the thermometer past 100°F in Hollywood, California, I found myself wondering if hell might just be a few degrees cooler than that first day of September in 1955.

After six weeks of apprentice training at Desilu Studios, I was on my way to my first day on a *real* job in the television industry, assisting the film editor on *I Love Lucy*. This was my big day. Between the nerves and the heat, I could feel the back of my shirt sticking to the seat of the 1955 Ford Victoria I had scrimped and saved for as I wheeled onto the lot at Cahuenga and Willoughby where some of Desilu's shows were filmed.

My dad was a banker, and none too thrilled when I passed on a business scholarship to Yale for show business. Oh, yeah—that went over big. After a year of working fulltime at Bank of America, I wanted to follow in the family business, all right.

Just not his business.

All three of Dad's brothers were employed in the entertainment industry. Sol London was studio manager at RKO Culver, Johnny London was the producer of *The Loretta Young Show*, and Louis London was a grip at Fox.

As a child, I spent many Saturday afternoons wandering around the RKO Culver Studios lot where they shot the legendary David O. Selznick classic, *Gone with the Wind*. This was spellbinding for a kid who loved to paint, draw cartoons, and ramble around with an old 35mm camera in hand, constantly experimenting with light and composition.

When not at the studio lot on the weekends, I could be found at the movie theater, completely lost in great classics such as *From Here to Eternity*, *The Wild One*, and my all-time favorite, *A Place in the Sun*, starring Elizabeth Taylor and the great Montgomery Clift.

By this time, I really had my heart set on becoming an art director, something my uncle at RKO was more than happy to help with but simply could not. In those days, if you didn't have a parent who was already an art director, you didn't have a shot at getting into the Guild. Enter the classic catch-22: To get a job, you had to be in the Guild. To be in the Guild, you had to get a job.

Uncle Sol broke the bad news to me one Saturday afternoon on the lot. "Look, Jerry," he said. "I'm not going to be able to get you a job in art direction. I'm sorry. But," he added, trying to soften the blow, "I can get you into film editing." Having clearly read the "what the heck is film editing?" expression on my face, he immediately headed across the lot to a cutting room with me numbly shuffling along behind.

The door opened on a little room whose floor was littered with a sea of bits and pieces of chopped-up film. Not exactly a canvas and brush, but it was a start. *Oh, well*, I sighed. *At least I'll be in show biz.* A clear path it wasn't, but it was the only path I had.

Before I knew it, I was hired and on my way to my new job. I could feel my banker father's furrowed brow of disapproval at my wrinkled and sweaty shirt from all the way across town as I wandered through the blistering heat looking for the editing rooms. Trying to ignore the knot in my stomach, I climbed the rickety metal stairs to the cutting rooms. I opened the door and made my way down a dark, narrow hallway. My gratitude to be out of the blazing sun was short lived as I quickly realized there was no air-conditioning in the old building.

"Well, hello there. I've been expecting you!" came a voice from the far end of the hall.

I froze, waiting for my eyes to adjust to the dark before heading down the corridor. The cramped room I'd just wandered into was filled with splicing machines, odd-looking tools, and a man standing before me stripped down to nothing but his underwear.

Expecting me?

I didn't know whether to laugh out loud or glance around the room for any available sharp object with which to defend myself. Maybe my dad was right after all—this business *was* full of crackpots!

We were still a long way from digital in those days. Film wound on large metal reels was edited by hand. Splicing was a laborious, low-tech process that consisted of using paperclips to attach two pieces of film together after scraping them and then brushing them with an acrid-smelling adhesive compound.

As there was no AC in those tiny, stuffy rooms, the gentleman standing before me in his skivvies, Bud Molin, editor of *I Love Lucy*—simply preferred to work in the stifling heat wearing as little as possible. Turns out Bud was a kind man with a gentle manner. I worked for him for two years and enjoyed every minute. Our strong working relationship resulted in an even stronger friendship, with Bud performing best man duties at my wedding.

It is here that the magic of the filmmaking began to unfold for me. I learned how the skill in which each tiny frame of film is edited into place makes such a huge impact on the final product. Editing, along with strong scripts, talented performers, and beautiful costumes are all assembled into the television shows and films that steal our hearts. I was hooked for life.

Little did I know that on that very first day I would be introduced to a law that governs the most frustrating and exhilarating moments in the film business: ALWAYS expect the unexpected!

Jerry (in the background) splicing film at Desilu 1955

JERRY LONDON

DESILU—RIGHT ON TRACK!

Lucy may have been the star of the show, but she was quick to credit Desi as being the brains behind their groundbreaking show, *I Love Lucy*, and the wildly successful production company, Desilu, that created it.

Desi was very hands on, so much so that he kept editing and screening equipment in each of their three homes. Their primary residence was in Beverly Hills, but they had a place in Palm Springs for when they felt like catching some desert sun, and another in Del Mar, which was most often occupied during the horse racing season.

As Desi always wanted to see the previous week's edits of the show, the routine was that every Saturday Bud and I packed up the film and hauled it out to whichever house Desi was currently staying at to screen them for him.

One Saturday, as Desi, Bud, and I were working away editing film on the old Moviola (dubbed "The Four-Headed Monster") in Desi's Del Mar garage, in strolled British-born Johnny Longden, the Triple Crown-winning jockey. Mr. Longden will forever be remembered by fans of *I Love Lucy*, having later made a guest appearance in one of the more memorable episodes called "Lucy and the Loving Cup," where Lucy gets her head stuck inside a trophy cup.

"It's your lucky day today, Desi," Johnny confidently boasted. "Today is the day I'm going to bring your horse in."

Desi gave him a long stare. Then, reaching over to the ashtray to crush out his cigarillo, he declared, "Okay boys, les wrap it up. We goin' to de track." Out the door we went.

Flying down the freeway with Desi behind the wheel of his shiny white Cadillac, listening to him chatting it up with his comrade Fernando Lamas in the front seat next to him, I sat in the back seat next to Bud, wondering how the heck "this new kid" had found himself here.

We were warmly greeted at the Del Mar racetrack and immediately escorted into the elite club boxes. High hopes and excited chatter from ladies dressed to the nines in big, showy hats and gentlemen in impeccable suits and silk ties filled the air. We feasted like kings while the finest scotch on the rocks tinkled in Desi's glass.

Finally, it was time for the big race. You could feel the anticipation as the horses were led into the starting gate for the sixth race. Not wanting to be dismissed as a naive kid in this sophisticated crowd, I put five bucks down on the nose on Desi's horse to win. A real chunk of change for me in those days, thank you very much.

The moment we heard the starter call, "And theeey're off," Desi sprang to his feet yelling, swearing, and screaming at his horse in some hybrid form of Spanish and English to "move his ass!"

Maybe racehorses understand Spanglish—I don't know—but believe it or not, Desi's horse charged across the finish line and won the race! Suddenly in the midst of all the boisterous, congratulatory backslapping, the inquiry flag went up. . . . There was a problem. It seems Desi's horse had bumped another horse on its ride to victory and could potentially be disqualified for it.

Desi came unglued. He launched into a cursing tirade the likes of which I had never heard in my life! Even cussing out the officials! I buried my face in my hands.

Time is a funny thing. Ten minutes earlier, I had been grinning from ear to ear, hardly able to believe my luck. I was being seen at the races with Desi Arnaz! Now I'm wanting the Earth to swallow me up.

The officials finally ruled "no interference," and Desi's horse was declared the official winner. Cheers went up all around and order was quickly restored.

We made our exit soon afterward to head back to Desi's place. This was, after all, still a workday. Fernando, comfortably seated in front for the ride back up to the house, leaned over to Desi and said, "Turn on the radio. I wanna hear the last race."

"Why?" Desi frowned suspiciously. "Did you have sonetin' special goin' in de ninth?"

"Jus' a longshot called Sky Blue Night," Fernando replied nonchalantly. "I put a coupl'a bucks on her, but you know why they call 'em longshots, eh?"

It was clear to even me that "a coupl'a bucks" translated to a few grand. When the race was announced, the chatter in the car stopped as we all listened intently.

"And the winner of the ninth and final race of the day . . . Sky Blue Night at fifty to one odds."

"I'm suppose' to be your fren, an' you dun't tell me abou dat horse???" Desi screamed.

Fernando just laughed.

What followed this time was pure Spanish between the two amigos.

I sat in the back seat gazing out the window at the setting sun, glad I didn't understand a single word!

CLASS IS IN

There was never a better classroom than Desilu for learning, and I was a walking sponge. I worked six days a week, and when my work was finished I poked around to see what else I could learn. I had asked Bud to let me edit some scenes, so by the time I was actually promoted to film editor, I had already cut a lot of film.

Add to that being able to slip down into the shadows of the *I Love Lucy* set a few times a week to watch rehearsals with comedy giants like Milton Berle, Bob Hope, and Red Skelton and . . . well, it made my two years on the show pass very quickly, leaving me eternally grateful for an education impossible to replicate.

Life was good, the studio camaraderie was great, and I loved my job.

Life got even more interesting when a friend of mine headed off to the army and tossed his "little black book" to another single buddy of mine. He quickly jumped on the newfound cache and scheduled himself a date with one of the girls in the book. Yep, she had a friend, so naturally he wanted me to come along with them on the date. Sure, why not?

The four of us met for coffee at a place on Sunset Boulevard near Vermont. There, I was introduced to the lovely Marilynn Landau. It wasn't long before the beautiful, sparkly, mischievous University of Southern California student managed to make all the fun I was having exploring my buddy's "little black book" not so much fun anymore.

After a particularly enchanting evening with Marilynn at an awards dinner at the Biltmore Hotel in downtown Los Angeles, I was totally hooked. A Thanksgiving Day proposal soon followed, and by the next June another new adventure in my life began called marriage.

(Fatherhood commenced a year later when my daughter Lisa was born.)

I was an assistant film editor with a steady job at that point in time, so neither Marilynn nor I had any way of knowing all the crazy travel that lay ahead. Marilynn is adventurous and adaptable, and I'm lucky I chose a girl with the fortitude to take this ride with me.

Jerry, Lucille Ball, and Marilynn at a Desilu Picnic 1956

HE HAS BIG PLANS FOR ME!

Needing eight years of experience to be promoted to full editor, I had a long way to go, but with nine different shows running simultaneously at Desilu, lots of opportunities existed. I was sent over to *The Danny Thomas Show* to edit it for syndication, which meant I had to remove three minutes from each episode. Learning to cut time out of the story while editing around the jokes and preserving the storyline was a brilliant exercise for a future director. I also assisted on *The Untouchables* with Robert Stack and *The Greatest Show on Earth*, a circus series starring Jack Palance.

I loved the work, and I was getting good at it. One of the other editors, an old-timer also doing the syndication job but hating it, asked me to do his editing for him and slipped me half his pay! I was actually working a job-and-a-half, with no one the wiser!

After eight years at Desilu, I finally made full editor. My very first show was *Glynis*, starring the British actress Glynis Johns. You would best know her as the mother of the three precocious Banks children in the beloved movie classic, *Mary Poppins*.

Ed Feldman was at the helm as producer of the *Glynis* show. I had come to know Ed while editing some commercials he'd produced.

My habit of working quickly drove my assistant nuts, with pieces of film flying faster than he could keep up. Ed, however, gave me the highest vote of confidence. My work continually gained his approval with a first pass and a "ship it," rarely if ever requiring any changes.

I was spared the angst of worrying about the next job when facing the sudden demise of that show. Thanks to my reputation, I got an offer from 20th Century Fox to edit *Daniel Boone*. Good thing, too, because I had put a down payment on our first house, where we welcomed our second child, Todd.

After three months at Fox, I got a call from my now-mentor, Ed Feldman. He was executive producer on a new show at Bing Crosby Productions.

"Jerry," he said, "I want you to edit a pilot for me."

"What? Aww, Ed, I got a wife, a new baby, a mortgage, and a steady job here. I'm happy." I thanked him, but politely declined.

"You have to listen to me, Jerry. I've got big plans for you," he pressed.

Ed was a man I had an enormous amount of respect for and trusted implicitly—a trust which time would prove was well placed—so off to Bing Crosby Productions I went.

The pilot they were trying to get off the ground was none other than *Hogan's Heroes*.

HOGAN AND OTHER HEROES

The producers were very late in getting this new pilot to CBS, so it was a real trial by fire to jump in on the race to finish it. After working a full week, we completed shooting on Friday. I received the dailies on Saturday. I worked day and night Saturday and Sunday—almost forty- eight hours straight. I came in Monday morning, added the drum music to the opening sequence, and screened it for the producers. In total, a ninety-hour work week! I had never worked so hard on anything.

The news was good—they loved it. Off to CBS the pilot went that afternoon, and by Wednesday we had a "go." I've since waited longer in lines for a coffee at Starbucks than for a green light on that show!

Hogan's Heroes was a hit right out of the box. I happily edited the first six episodes. Then Ed decided he wanted to move me up to be his assistant producer.

At the time, I had a guy by the name of Michael Kahn as my assistant in the editing room. When I moved up, it meant I would leave my position as editor to him.

"You're moving up to full editor, Mike," I told him.

Having only been an assistant editor for about six months, Mike was reluctant. "But I don't know anything about editing," he said anxiously.

"C'mon, Mike, you'll have the easiest job in the world. All you have to do is edit the footage for me. I'll tell you how to fix it, then we'll run it for the producers. You have nothing to worry about."

And I was right.

Mike did a fantastic job and the rest, as we all know, is cinematic history. With his Emmy and Academy Awards still accumulating, I would of course like to think I taught him everything he knows about editing, but I'm pretty sure Steven Spielberg would have something to say about that! Mike went on to work with the legendary director, which resulted in one of the most extraordinarily successful collaborations in the history of filmmaking.

As assistant to the producer, I had my hands in everything—script readings, reviewing the editing, props, wardrobe, casting . . . I was everywhere, learning everything I could. I even cast the minor roles. A better film school simply does not exist.

With very funny scripts and a cast skillfully nailing punchlines, it's no wonder the show ran for six seasons. Richard Dawson possessed that dry British wit that always had me in stitches. Bob Crane, a laid-back kind of guy, had a drum kit set up in his dressing room that he played just for fun between takes. John Banner put up a good front for his imaginary diet, but he had a weak spot for sweets and was forever sneaking them into his dressing room. Robert Clary, who played Frenchman Corporal Louis LeBeau, had an infectious energy that everyone adored.

Aside from a nearly impossible-to-ignore undercurrent of animosity between John Banner, who got the laughs as Sergeant Schultz, and Werner Klemperer, who won the Emmys as Colonel Klink, the set was a fun, easy, loose, low-pressure good time.

Jerry, actress Marlyn Mason, and Ed Feldman

Bob Crane and Jerry

Jerry with The Heroes

ED FELDMAN, MENTOR

As the second season rolled along with a parade of guest directors, Ed Feldman finally decided he'd like to try his hand at directing. He wanted me and my "editor's eye" right there with him, to help ensure he got all the angles, etc. Lucky for me, my suggestions such as turning the camera in a different direction to gain depth of field—a technique gleaned from behind my little 35mm camera lens as a kid—were welcomed and actively applied.

I was very young, and grateful to be employed in work I loved, so I didn't think much about tomorrow. In fact, I didn't think about it at all. Until one day my mentor Ed told me, "With your talent, Jerry, it's time for you to start thinking about making a career decision. Producing or directing?" This was truly the first time I had ever given a thought about directing.

Not long after that seed was planted, he mentioned that if I was interested in directing, I might consider doing an episode of *Hogan's Heroes*.

Wow. A hit show, comic greats, and now I was being ASKED to direct! How could it get better than this?

So naturally, I said no.

I wasn't ready, and I knew it. I didn't have the confidence or the skills to do it. Not that I wasn't intrigued—a challenge was always a call to arms for me. Besides, with a growing family at home, I realized Ed was right; my career had better keep growing, too.

For one thing, staging baffled me. For another, I had never really worked directly with actors. I wouldn't call myself a "cautious" person by any means, but failure was not an option for me, and I figured out pretty early on that anything can happen on a set. The director is the captain of the ship, the commander in chief, the head honcho, and when calamity strikes—and, oh, will it ever—the director is the person everyone turns to for the answers.

I started spending more and more time on the set, and learned blocking by watching the guest directors. I found myself picking the brains of the likes of Bob Sweeney, Mark Daniels, and Gene Reynolds. Gene had a great piece of advice to help guide me through blocking: Always try to bring motion into a scene, and let the dialogue guide you through the blocking. He was generous in his explanations of the various intricacies of staging. And he was spot on. Getting good movement into the dialogue is inherent to an interesting piece of film, and it was an approach I set out to master.

Noting that videotape technology was rising in the television industry, I also decided to up my tech skills. I enrolled in a night course at USC to learn the finer details of shooting in that medium.

So, tech update . . . check.

Camera angles . . . check.

Blocking . . . check.

Composition . . . check.

Was I ready? Not quite. There was still one tiny element I needed to know more about.

Actors.

ACTORS AND OTHER STRANGERS

Having participated in a good deal of the casting process and observing the way various guest directors addressed the talent, I realized there was a special way to talk to actors that I didn't yet have a handle on. So, off to an actor's workshop I went.

Two nights a week, I was at Theater East, directing scenes in everything from the stellar comedies of Neil Simon to the serious drama of Tennessee Williams' masterpiece, *A Streetcar Named Desire*. It was a fantastic learning experience because the actors critiqued my scenes. Realizing how beneficial these critiques were, I enrolled in a drama class at UCLA, as well.

It was through this process that the value of rehearsals was driven home. I would always ask for table reading of the script with all my actors going forward; it was here that I got to listen to the dialogue for the first time and find out what worked and what didn't.

I also came to realize there was more to directing actors than simply instructing them on when and where you want them to move. It dawned on me that a complete connection between actor and director was built upon a special kind of trust. I could see that this complex relationship was one I needed a better understanding of. What is directing without good communication, and what is good communication without truly understanding the person you are trying to reach?

Figuring this was the missing link, I enrolled in a night class in psychology at Santa Monica City College, which I attended for two years. It was indeed the most important course I ever took.

Because of the fast pace of television shoots, there is seldom adequate time for actors and directors to really get to know each other. Finding a point of connection with any one person is tricky, but necessary to establish that needed rapport. The best results come when an actor truly trusts his director. It definitely shows on the screen.

Little did I know at the time that those psych classes would be the most valuable tools in my toolbox, that the path before me would be not only brimming with generous, kind, easygoing, polished professionals, but also riddled with vastly overinflated egos, drug addicts, sex addicts, narcissists, alcoholics, and neurotics of every age, gender, and breed—some of the most infinitely talented Oscar, Tony, and Emmy Award-winning talent to ever step in front of a camera.

Yep, to say the psych courses proved to be useful in my career would be putting it rather mildly!

We were in the middle of the fourth season of *Hogan's Heroes*. Now finally feeling confident enough to put it all together, I went to Ed and uttered the fateful words, "I'm ready to direct."

He assigned the last show of the fourth season to me. Nerves ran headlong into solid preparation. I knew where to move the cameras, where to move the actors, and where to move the director! It went as smooth as glass.

The fifth season opened with a promotion to associate producer. I also directed four episodes in that season and five episodes in the sixth, which pretty much made me a regular director in the rotation.

THIS IS THE ABBY

*H*ogan's Heroes* ran for six years. Then THAT day arrived—the one you know will come along eventually, but keep the thought of neatly shelved in the deepest recesses of your mind.

The show was finally canceled, leaving me jobless for the first time in fifteen years with a wife, a mortgage, and two kids.

Enter the dark side of show business—the troubling thoughts during the day about where in the world you're going to find another job and the tormenting visions in the middle of the night about what will happen if you don't.

The price I was now paying for having been happily ensconced in a regular gig? My connections had become pretty lean.

I managed to scratch around and shoot some commercials here and there to keep going until one day good ol' Ed Feldman stepped in again, this time to offer me a position as associate producer on *The Doris Day Show*.

"This is not going to be like *Hogan's Heroes*, Jerry. I can't even promise you'll get to direct," he warned me. "It's different. This is the movie star, Doris Day."

I wasn't exactly sure what he meant by "different," but I soon found out. It was indeed a very different set from *Hogan's Heroes*, and nowhere near as much fun. Aside from the presence of Doris' beloved dogs on the set—she was always urging us to adopt strays—that ship was run very tightly. Don't get me wrong. I was grateful for the job. But Doris Day was the boss. As star, executive producer, and with her name on the marquee, America's sweetheart was in control, with a firm grip.

Nevertheless, I still got to direct a couple of episodes. Ed had come through again.

Jerry and Doris Day

It was there that I had the great fortune to meet the legendary production manager, Abby Singer. This was the man for whom the standard industry term, "This is the Abby," (which means "the next to the last shot before a wrap") was named. Abby knew everybody in the business, so to get noticed by him with a fortuitous, "Hey you're good. Why aren't you directing more?" was a big deal.

Abby was extremely helpful in my career path; he's the one who introduced me to Paramount and Columbia Studios. He was instrumental in getting me over to *The Brady Bunch* for four or five episodes, where I had a wonderful time. Sherwood Schwartz produced not only *The Brady Bunch*, but also hits like *Gilligan's Island*. His son, Lloyd, (an associate producer on those shows) and I were about the same age, so I really enjoyed working with both him and his father.

I owe such a debt of gratitude to Abby Singer. My career might never have unfolded the way it did without his support.

Soon I was over at *The Partridge Family*. I had worked with kids before on *The Brady Bunch* and, as intimidating as the old adage is about working with kids and dogs, directing kids was really pretty easy.

Then there was Danny Bonaduce.

What a handful. He was a real-life Dennis the Menace. He earned every bit of his precocious reputation. I understand he still gets well paid for being a smart-ass on the radio!

David Cassidy, who played the eldest son, Keith, in the show, was in real life Shirley Jones' stepson by way of her marriage to his father, Jack Cassidy. Actor, musician, and heartthrob, David was an absolute machine. The guy worked all week long filming the show in L.A., then jumped on a plane every weekend to God-knows-where to perform live, then was back on the set Monday morning. There were always plenty of girls around to wear him out, too. That kid never rested. I honestly don't know how he did it.

Academy Award winner Shirley Jones was a doll and a dream to work with. However, America's TV mom, Mrs. Partridge, was not without her spice.

One day I had a question for her and knocked on her trailer door.

"Come in," she chirped through the door, so I opened it and went on in. There she was going about her business . . . topless.

There went that question right out of my head, as well as anything that even slightly resembled the English language. I excused myself and made a hasty retreat, telling her we'd talk later.

She was one hot mama, I can tell you that. Never did remember that question!

Jerry and Shirley Jones

25

SID CAESAR WITH LOVE

Soon I found myself at Paramount directing episodes of the show *Love American Style*, which was structured as two or three different short stories per episode. There was no regular cast, but with such stellar writing, there was always a parade of amazing talent passing through the set.

One particularly memorable episode starred the legendary comedic icon from *Your Show of Shows*, Sid Caesar. I was thrilled and a bit nervous when I tapped on the door of his trailer to introduce myself the morning of the shoot.

"Hey kid! Come on in," he said, motioning me into his trailer. "It's great to meet you. I've got a few ideas on the script. Have a seat."

It was already a pretty funny script about a guy getting a bowling ball stuck on his thumb after his wife forbids him to bowl, so I was thinking a couple of tweaks couldn't hurt—this was *the* Sid Caesar, after all. An hour later, I emerged from his trailer with a whole new script! He'd rewritten the whole damn thing, and you know what? It was funnier! Problem is, the other actors who had been cast were rehearsed and standing by, ready to shoot. But what was I gonna do, say "no" to Sid Caesar? This left me with no choice but to go to the producer and tell him I had a whole new script.

"So how are you going to get the day's work done, Jerry?" came the producer's stern voice at the other end of the telephone.

"Don't worry," I said, trying not to sound panicky. "It'll get done."

"And what about the guest stars?" he pressed.

"Let's just get this thing typed up and I'll figure something out," I responded, trying to sound more convinced than I actually was.

By 10:00 a.m. the crew members, who were just standing around, started asking me what I was planning to do.

"Improvise, of course," I said confidently. Can't have the captain of the ship looking like he's expecting a mutiny, now can you?

At 11:00, still no script. At 11:30 we finally got the new script and started blocking and rehearsing, but the lunch break was looming large and still not a frame of film had been shot.

At noon, the huge studio doors swung open and, with backlighting only a chief lighting tech could dream up, into the dark studio perfectly silhouetted in the bright daylight behind them walked the Big Cheeses. Three of the suits from the head office upstairs were here, and they were gunning for me.

"Jerry, it's 12:00 and you haven't even starting rolling yet," they started.

"How are you going to finish this in two days?" they probed.

"Don't worry, I'll get it done," I said again, having absolutely no idea how I was going to pull this off.

With a pretty good handle on staging, I blocked out and rehearsed seven pages in one shot, weaving among the single, two-shot, and master cameras.

Sid Caesar, Jerry, and Kathleen Nolan on *Love American Style*

There would be many more times that my editing experience saved my ass.

We had come back from lunch having still not rolled a single frame of film. But by the end of the day, I had miraculously shot my ten pages, and was back on schedule.

Day two ended with another thirteen pages shot, and we wrapped the episode on time. The integrity of the script was all there and it turned out to be very funny.

This is what happens when you don't panic and allow experience, confidence, blind faith, and a good stiff scotch on the rocks at the end of the day to merge from one hell of a challenge into a damned good show!

THREE-CAMERA COMEDIES

For about five years I bounced around Paramount working on sitcoms. I shot an early *Happy Days*, which was another wonderfully warm set, *The Brady Bunch* (... oh, and no. I did not witness any Mrs. Robinson-type action between Florence Henderson and Barry Williams), and many more episodes of *Love American Style*.

Shortly thereafter, the producers asked me if I knew three-camera show technique. Yes, of course I knew three-camera show technique, I told them. Owing to my work on *I Love Lucy*, the first three-camera show ever (thanks to Desi Arnaz, who was way ahead of his time), I was very familiar with it.

Had they asked if I had ever directed using this technique ... hmm ... well, that's an entirely different question, now isn't it?

Before long, I found myself directing an episode of *The Paul Lynde Show* with star Paul Lynde, a funny guy with a quick but acerbic wit. The show was—you guessed it—a three-camera show, so I figured that once again I'd think my way out of things. Happily, it turns out I knew where to place the cameras. Apparently, I had absorbed more than I realized while editing three-camera shows at *I Love Lucy*. Enough to get asked back.

I soon found myself on two other three-camera shows, *The Mary Tyler Moore Show* and *The Bob Newhart Show*, thanks once again to mentor Abby Singer.

The Newhart Show was an absolute dream job. Not only was the material great, Bob was the perfect combination of naturally funny and easygoing. Suzanne Pleshette, who had a mouth on her that would make a sailor blush, was truly one of the funniest women I have ever known.

Mary Tyler Moore and Jerry

One day, as I wandered over to craft services to get a cup of coffee, I accidentally overheard series regular Marcia Wallace and Suzanne deep in a discussion about some guy—or rather some guy's anatomy—with explicitly detailed descriptions of the appearance and, shall we say, usage of said appendage. Just when I was trying to figure out how to make an undetected exit to save everyone a mortifying "Please God Let the Floor Open and Swallow Me Whole" moment, they revealed that my "accidental" eavesdrop wasn't an accident at all! It had been gleefully orchestrated by both ladies, who burst into fits of hysterical laughter at my embarrassment!

The usual routine on that show was almost too good to be true. We didn't start the work week until Tuesday, when we came in to read and rewrite the script. We would review the rewrite and block on Wednesday and Thursday, shoot on Friday, and take a three-day weekend.

Suzanne Pleshette, Jerry, and Bob Newhart

In spite of the cushy gig on a comedy show, I found myself itching more and more to do drama. Expressions to my agent of such desires always led back to, "Sorry Jer. You're known in this town as a comedy director." I persisted, but it was always the same. "Look, if you just had some dramatic film . . ." I was haunted by that refrain.

So there it was again—the eternal catch-22 we are forever hearing actors complain about. "How can I get a dramatic roll if I only get cast in comedies?" Well, how could I direct a dramatic film if I only got hired for comedies? How could I get into drama? Don't get me wrong. I was very grateful to be employed and respected as a comedy director, but that little voice inside my head kept pushing me to do drama. *Maybe*, I thought, *I should just shut the hell up and count my blessings*. But that little voice had other ideas.

It is an often-overlooked fact in life that only sometimes opportunities present themselves. Other times . . . you have to create them.

A Comedy Godfather

I was reading over a *Love American Style* script I'd just received, an episode that was a comedic riff on the cinematic masterpiece, *The Godfather*. There was that little voice in my head again, only this time it had morphed into a much louder little devil on my shoulder, with some pretty good ideas up its sleeve.

"Shoot this as a drama. Don't punch the close-ups, use more camera movement. C'mon, Jer, ya know you want to. You know you can do it." On and on that voice urged. Persuasive little guy. In the end, the siren song of a creative challenge was too strong for me to resist.

The next day on the set I pulled my assistant director and director of photography aside for a chat. "Look," I said. "I want to do this one really differently. I want low-key lighting, rack focuses, you know, shoot it like a drama."

"What will the producers think?" my assistant director said after a long "have-you-lost-your-mind" stare. "What if they don't like it, Jerry?"

"Well, then, I guess they just won't use me again." I shrugged, pumped up by that creative devil on my shoulder.

They went along with my plan, and the set looked amazing.

The actor cast for this episode, Nehemiah Persoff, had great dramatic acting chops. They served to further my renegade ways by making it that much easier to push ahead with my "dramatic concept" of this comedy show. He was brilliant.

We shot for three days. I found myself breaking a bit of a sweat each evening when the dailies arrived. The producers, having likely been looking for nothing more than if all the lines on the script were spoken—they were—and if the jokes worked—they did—were very complimentary. I finished shooting and editing. I had a ball accomplishing my covert mission, and that was the end of that.

Or so I thought.

About six weeks later, in a stack of mail on my desk at home, I came across a letter from ABC executive Tony Barr, who served as head of programing for the network. I never got mail from the network, so I nervously opened and read the letter. It coldly informed me that Mr. Barr had seen an episode of *Love American Style* that I had directed and wanted to talk to me about it. I was instructed to make an appointment to see him at his office in Century City.

Well, the jig's up now, I thought. Not only did I screw myself out of work at Paramount, I likely screwed myself out of work at an entire network!

Three long days later and what seemed an even longer wait in the outer office on the twelfth floor of an imposing Century City high rise, I was finally ushered into the "big office" to see Mr. Barr face to face.

"Have a seat," he said, pointing to a large leather armchair chair that faced his baronial desk. "Would you like some coffee?"

Feeling that even water would go down like molten lava over the grinding knots in my stomach, I respectfully declined.

"I'm familiar with your reputation directing comedies like *Hogan's Heroes*, but I just saw an episode of *Love American Style* that you directed."

Oh, boy. Here it comes.

"I've seen hundreds of episodes of that show. It's part of my job," he continued. "I've got to say, yours was the most original work I've seen. I want to tell you how much I enjoyed your camera work."

If there hadn't been arms on that big leather chair, I would surely have fallen to the floor.

"Really?? Uh, well, thank you," my stunned brain managed to stammer. "I really enjoyed doing it."

"I wanted to meet with you so I could tell you myself," he said, leaning back in his chair. "So what do you want to do, Jerry?"

"I really want to direct drama, Mr. Barr. That's why I shot it that way," I responded.

"So, why aren't you?" he asked, appearing genuinely perplexed.

"Because I'm considered a "comedy director." I shrugged.

"Aww, c'mon." He laughed as he reached for the phone and started dialing.

After some chitchat my addled brain wasn't entirely focused on, he put the phone down and redirected his attention to me. "That was Dave O'Connell, the producer of the one-hour drama *Marcus Welby, MD* over at

Universal. You're going to go meet him." He stated this matter-of-factly, and just like that our meeting was over.

I floated out of the building with my feet barely touching the ground! The roll of the dice had paid off!

Six weeks after our initial meeting, I found myself on the set of *Marcus Welby, MD*, preparing to direct my very first drama. I was ecstatic to once again wake up and realize I was living the experience I had repeatedly fantasized about in my head. The day had finally arrived, and the scrawny young kid from Alhambra was ready to start his next big adventure!!

I got the script, start prepping, and headed to the set to introduce myself to the very pleasant Robert Young, who starred as Dr. Marcus Welby, and the boyishly handsome James Brolin, who played his protégé, Dr. Steven Kiley.

About ten minutes into the spiel about my ideas for shooting this episode, James interrupted. "Who are you again?" he asked, looking puzzled.

"Uhh, I'm the director of the episode you're about to shoot," I sputtered.

"Oh yeah, yeah. Oh, I'm sorry, I'm sorry," he said sheepishly. "I apologize."

Lest one ever fly a little too close to the sun in this industry, there will always be someone or something to bring you back down to Earth!

A couple of days into the shoot, Jim popped by early to see me on the set. "Here, this is for you," he said, tossing a bag into my lap.

Inside the bag, I found a red sweatshirt with large, gold lettering across the chest that read, "Jerry London." On the back, it said, "I Am the Director."

"Just in case I forget again," he said with a wink, and we both burst into laughter.

Not only did I wear that sweatshirt, shortly after the shoot I decided to grow a beard to try to look older!

In the subsequent years, Tony Barr and I became good friends. Aside from being ABC's head of current programming, he also ran an acting class. He asked me over several times to speak to the actors. I was more than happy to do this, in order to repay Tony in some small way for his faith in me.

Robert Young, Jerry, and James Brolin

THIRTY-SIX HOURS IN TWO YEARS

There were so many hit television shows being produced at Universal Studios at that time that efficiency was essential to maintain the pace of the workload. To that end, there was a certain "book" the studios kept on all of the directors working on their productions. This book logged exactly how many hours they spent shooting their shows, mostly noting whether they came in on time or went overtime. Any director going over the allotted time received a black mark in the book.

Word got around that I never went over and that my timing was down pat. The results of this were that I found myself in great demand at Universal. In my entire career, I never once compromised quality for speed; it was simply my natural pace. I never consciously intended to wrap ahead of time; I was just blessed with the skill to do it. Producers also liked the way I staged scenes and my choices of camera angles, both of which contributed to a story well told.

I moved around the lot from one hour-long show to another. I directed *Six Million Dollar Man*, *Marcus Welby, MD*, *Rockford Files*, and *Kojak*. In total, I directed thirty-six one-hour-long, six-day shoots in a two-year period.

And what a rewarding two years they were.

The shows at Universal were as diverse as the actors who starred in them.

Lee Majors, star of *Six Million Dollar Man*, was another very pleasant guy to work with. Good thing, because the show was loaded with stunts, which could sometimes be taxing.

One day we had a particularly risky stunt that called for a character to jump off a rock of pretty significant height into a lake on the backlot at Universal Studios. I voiced my misgivings about the precariousness of the jump with the experienced stuntman, and was quickly dismissed with the requisite "I do this stuff all the time" bravado.

Okay, then, roll 'em.

He made the jump into the lake just fine. He just didn't come up afterwards.

Thirty or forty of the longest seconds of my life passed, and when it was clear he wasn't coming up, the stunt crew jumped in to find him and drag him out. He had apparently hit his head on a rock down below and been knocked unconscious. Miraculously, the guy survived with nothing more than a minor concussion, but I needed to change my underwear!

Hawaii Five-O was a blast because both times I directed it were just before or after a holiday. It was such a drag to be "stuck" in Hawaii for three weeks!

I met the fabulous Cliff Gorman there who had just finished doing *Lennie* on Broadway, and also cast Edward James Olmos in a bit part early in his career. He was so good that I actively searched for roles for him in everything I did thereafter. Fantastic actor. Both Cliff and Eddie became lifelong friends of mine.

Rockford Files was another great time. Stephen Cannell's scripts and staff were always top-notch. Producer Charles Johnson, another terrific guy, really believed in me, which made my job even easier.

Then there was James Garner.

I can't say enough about what a super guy James Garner was, and what superb acting chops he possessed. He'd give me a great take on a scene, then ask if he could do another. I was happy with the first take, but sure, why not? That guy could do four completely different takes on any one scene and they'd *all* be good! The only thing that frustrated this incredibly even-tempered man was a bum knee that prevented him from doing some of his own stunts.

That and Producer Glen Larson.

JUST IN CASE YOU MISSED IT

We were starting a night shoot on a *Rockford Files* on the rooftop of a building widely known as "The Black Tower" over at Universal when I noticed that Jim was unusually preoccupied. After observing numerous chats between him and my assistant director, I called the AD over to find out what was going on. Was Jim having a problem of some kind that I should be aware of?

Nope, no problem.

The AD explained that Jim wanted to speak to Glen Larson. So Jim had asked Scotty, the longtime guard down at the front gate, to detain Glen when he passed the gate on his way home for the night until Jim came down. Jim then asked the AD to keep in touch with Scotty and let him know the second Glen got there.

No big deal. We went back to shooting.

Before long, Jim politely excused himself and disappeared.

A bit of background on this: Producer Glen Larson had quite a reputation for, shall we say, "borrowing" ideas from existing movies and hit TV shows and putting them into his shows as his own. He was so broadly known for his piracy that he earned himself the nickname of "Glen Larceny" in the television industry.

It seems that complaints to and fines from the Writers Guild didn't prove to be much of a deterrent to Glen, nor did they give Jim the satisfaction he was looking for—most particularly when Mr. Larson went on to "borrow" the theme music from the *Rockford Files* for one of his pilots. Well, let's just say ol' even-tempered Jim had had just about enough.

What unfolded at the gate that evening went like this: When Glen pulled up to the exit, Scotty asked if he would hold on for a minute because Jim Garner wanted to see him. When Jim got the word through my AD that Glen was at the gate, he shot down there in a flash and ordered Glen to roll down his window. When Glen complied, Jim reached in and punched him right in the face!

Jim looked back at the stunned guard, who was standing a few feet behind him. "Hey Scotty, did you see that?"

"Uhhh, no. No, sir. I didn't see anything, Mr. Garner, sir," stammered Scotty.

"Well, okay then. Watch this!" Jim hauled off and punched Glen again!

Suffice it to say, Jim returned to the set a little fired up and sporting a really big smile, then carried on like nothing had ever happened.

Jerry and James Garner

Telly the Slave Trader

Working on the mega hit show *Kojak* with Telly Savalas was a real adventure.

Telly possessed a photographic memory. He would take one look at a scene in the script and know it instantly. Furthermore, he never rehearsed. We'd even block the scene with his stand-in. When he came on set, you would slap the pages in his hand—which was probably the first time he'd ever seen them. After scanning the script, he'd pipe up with a quick, "Okay, where do you want me?" He'd be shown his marks, and then just do the entire scene, knowing every line and hitting every mark. Just like that. It was unbelievable! A real no-nonsense professional. He didn't believe in wasting any time on the set.

He didn't believe in wasting any time with the ladies, either.

Telly was enjoying wild popularity at the height of *Kojak*. At the end of each and every day, at 5:00 p.m. there were always three very attractive women waiting for him. Off he would go with all three. Always three. Never the same three. There was no "type," either. They were always diverse—bookish, Indian, athletic, African American, blonde, and on and on. Always different. Always three.

Every. Single. Day.

Telly's colossal popularity wasn't nearly as much fun for the rest of us as it clearly was for Telly.

I shot a two-hour episode of *Kojak* on location in New York City, which costarred Eli Wallach, F. Murray Abraham, Jerry Orbach, and Michael Gazzo from *The Godfather*. Dream cast and excellent script.

Much of the shoot consisted of exteriors, which included some fantastic rooftop chases. Telly was so popular that the crowds in the street scenes were always yelling his name, so we ended up with a lousy soundtrack and had to loop everything in the studio.

Even doing car scenes with the camera mounted beside the driver's window resulted in most of the shots being ruined by people waving at Telly as he drove by. The telltale bald head was a dead giveaway to the driver's identity every time.

One day as I was standing on the street in Brooklyn setting up Telly's next scene, I heard a loud voice rise from the crowd behind me. "Oh, I can't wait to see Telly and that bald head of his! He makes me so hot!"

I turned to see a large black lady with her hair tied up in a red bandana practically jumping out of her shoes with excitement. When we were finally ready to shoot and Telly was called to the set, I looked toward his trailer. All I could see were hundreds and hundreds of women's hands raised as he walked by, hoping to get a touch of his head when he passed. As he approached the set, I suddenly heard the lady behind me shriek, "There he is! There's Telly!! Oooo-wee, am I gonna take it out on my ol' man tonight!"

The cast for that particular episode included a beautiful girl who had a small role as a sexy secretary. She was so good-looking that when she walked down the street even women's heads would turn.

Her first day on the set, Telly wasted no time getting the 411 on this girl. "So who's that?" he asked, eyeing the redheaded beauty.

"Who, Debbie? Oh, she's the girl I cast to play the secretary," I told him.

"Very nice, very nice," he said with a lingering eye, before wandering off.

Several days into the shoot, Telly pulled me aside for a chat. "Hey, Jerry. I asked Debbie if she'd go out with me and she said no," he confided with more than a trace of astonishment. "Can you help me out?"

"Geez, Telly, she's just an actress I cast. I can't really help you out in that area," I said, shaking off the request as best I could.

For the entire ten-plus-day shoot, he apparently tried to get a date with this girl to no avail, and it was really eating at him.

Toward the end of the shoot, Telly sidled up to me again, this time with a different strategy. "Have you noticed that at the end of the day there have been some pretty nice-looking women here?" he asked proudly.

"Yes, Telly. You'd have to be blind not to notice!" I laughed.

"Tomorrow there's going to be a gorgeous brunette waiting here. A five-foot ten-inch knockout. A former Miss New Jersey."

"Really? Wow, no kidding!" I said.

"Yeah, really! And she's yours," he whispered.

"What??" I was stunned.

"Yeah, yeah, she's for you. All you have to do is get Debbie to go out with me."

"Nah, gee thanks, Telly. I'm happily married." I wondered if there was now a red sweatshirt with my name in gold lettering on the front and the words, "I'm the Pimp" on the back.

Naturally, I said nothing to the actress—who incidentally never did go out with him—but sure enough the leggy brunette beauty he'd promised appeared the following day right on schedule at 5:00 sharp. Off she went—arm in arm with Telly.

Like I said, a real adventure!

Telly and Jerry in New York

JERRY LONDON

FROM *I LOVE LUCY* TO *SHŌGUN*... AND BEYOND

BARETTA, BLAKE, AND BRIDGES

I directed a couple episodes of *Baretta* during that period, too. Well . . . sort of. *Baretta* was a show about a tough-guy rogue cop, starring Robert Blake. Although it was masterfully written and produced by the talented Emmy Award-winning Stephen Cannell, there wasn't a single script that reached the hands of Robert Blake that he wouldn't tear to shreds with rewrites. While Blake was good at what he did in front of the camera, his constant revisions not only made it very hard on the other actors who had rehearsed the scenes as written, but drastically slowed the pace of the entire production, as well. So much so that after surviving the first excruciating cut-and-paste shoot, the time needed to get the second episode shot simply ran out. The studio had to drop my second episode.

Lloyd Bridges, at the extreme other end of the spectrum, was a consummate gentleman and a polished professional. Time would eventually teach me that the greater the talent, the easier they are to work with. Good actors can make work not only easy but also a true delight. This isn't to say that all situations with good actors are easy.

We were shooting on location in the middle of downtown Los Angeles one day on the set of *Joe Forrester*, a crime drama starring Lloyd Bridges, when Lloyd fell ill and had to leave. The work, however, still had to get done, so now what? The star of the show had just left and I had five pages to shoot by the end of the day.

With my steadfast belief that I could think my way out of any mess, I decided to dress the stand-in in Lloyd's wardrobe and proceed with filming all the long shots and over-the-shoulder tight shots. By the end of the day, I had crafted a complete day's work with no star. When Lloyd returned two days later, I shot the close-ups and, *bam*, we were done on time. This episode had the added distinction of featuring Sal Mineo from *Rebel Without a Cause* as a guest star.

SALAD OR GARBAGE?

They say the difference between salad and garbage is timing. Lucky for me, a part of the professional success I have enjoyed is due to that mysterious element of timing.

Television, since its inception, had really never strayed from its limited confines, mostly because formats for newscasts, situation comedies, variety shows, and dramas were borrowed from radio. Television's production, talent, and content were geared exclusively for TV sets and the living rooms they resided in.

Until the early 1970s, movies remained the exclusive domain of the cinema. In fact, so nonexistent were movies on television that when they did begin to appear, it was with the label, "Made-for-TV Movies." Lucky for us all, that period opened the door of filmmaking for creative young talent the likes of Steven Spielberg with his 1971 TV movie, *Duel.*

On a creative level, I found the movie format to be much more gratifying than series television. More time, bigger name actors, and best of all, independence. By and large, the producers rather than the director are the creative force in series television. Week after week, producers monitor the continuity of the feel of each show, while a parade of directors revolve in and out of episodic television. Movies, on the other hand, put the director in the driver's seat, giving them creative freedom.

Television was poised to flex its financial muscle by developing good scripts and shelling out for big-name talent. When the opportunity to direct a TV movie came about, I was primed and ready to go.

I realized then that I was standing on the edge of the Wild West.

MOVIES OF THE WEEK AND THE GERB

The Made-for-TV Movies format began taking over television in the '70s, and I got the call.

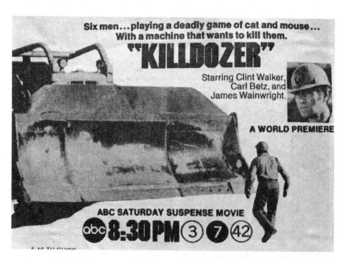

Killdozer

51

A heavy sci-fi thriller called *Killdozer* was my first TV movie. An all-male cast starring Robert Urich, Clint Walker, and Carl Betz told the story of a malevolent bulldozer on a killing rampage ala Spielberg's *Duel*. I loved the format and the broader creative license I had with movies, and couldn't wait to do more.

Fortunately, I didn't have to wait long.

Swan Song—David Soul

I was challenged again to think on my feet—or in this case on my ass—in Sun Valley, Idaho, for a Movie of the Week called *Swan Song*, starring David Soul. It was based on a true story about a champion skier pulling out of the Olympics due to a mystery illness. Needless to say, both snow and skiing would be involved, neither of which I am even remotely fond. I made that fact no secret to the studio, but with profuse reassurances and promises of my own personal ski instructor, I agreed to do it.

The instructor was a fearless, expert skier. After spending two straight days working on the slopes with the guy, I had that snowplow thing down pat.

On the third day, after declaring me perfectly adept at skiing and ready to master the mountain, he took me up the chairlift to the top of the highest peak.

Then he left me there.

Yeah, I know. You've never heard that one before, have you?

Clearly not cut from the same adrenaline-junkie cloth my instructor was, I spent the next hour and a half sliding down the mountain on my butt. So naturally, I did what any tenacious, not-easily-deterred fellow in my ski boots would do.

I spent the entire shoot going up and down the mountain in a snowcat.

On a sad footnote, it seems my instructor's daredevil ways did not ultimately serve him well. He was killed in a tragic skiing accident less than a year later.

Even as TV movie assignments picked up, I continued doing TV series. I simply loved to work.

I directed an episode of *Police Woman* starring Angie Dickinson. Angie remains one of my favorite actresses of all time and one of the nicest people I have ever worked with.

Police Story was also a cop show—this was a very popular genre at the time—which starred the irascible David Janssen.

We were shooting late on a Friday night in a parking garage in downtown Los Angeles. After returning from the dinner break (which had apparently included some adult beverages), David approached me while we were setting up the next shot. "I'm going home," he said. "I don't like this scene, and you don't need me in it."

"Hang on a second, David. I do need you! You're in the next scene," I shot back.

"I don't have to be in it. Just give my lines to the other actors," he growled over his shoulder as he marched off.

"I can't do that," I said, thinking quickly. "Just let me call the producer, David Gerber."

"Fine. Call him!" he snarled. He turned and walked with me toward the phone.

Anxious to get this scene wrapped up before the clock struck midnight and budget-busting Golden Time (triple pay) kicked in, I asked my assistant to run ahead of us over to the phone booth (pre-cellphone days) and start dialing.

"Hey Jer! How's it going?" the upbeat, funny, loquacious, and highly caffeinated voice of David Gerber greeted me. Gerber, our executive producer, reminded me of a Damon Runyon-type character out of *Guys and Dolls*. He was likable, tenacious as hell, and a really nice guy.

"Well, we've got a little problem, David," I said, trying hard not to sound too perturbed. "We're near the end of the day here, and Janssen doesn't want to be in the scene we're about to shoot. He says he's going home."

"Are you kidding? Ohhh, put him on the phone!" came David's buoyant response.

Janssen grabbed the phone with a snort. "Dave, it's Janssen," he barked into the receiver. "The scene is a piece of crap, they don't need me in it, I'm leaving." With that, he dropped the phone, leaving it dangling from its cord, jumped in a waiting limo, and screeched off.

After an exchange of blank stares with my assistant, I picked up the still-swinging phone to hear Gerber continuing to try and resolve the situation.

". . . this is important business now, David. You know you've got to be in this scene," chirped Dave in his best cheerleading tone.

"Gerb," I interrupted.

"Listen, David, you're not going to leave. C'mon. It's just another couple of shots." Mr. Gerber was on a roll.

"Gerb!" I tried again a little louder.

"Look," he went on, still completely oblivious, "I know it's been a long week, but you're almost done. Then you can . . ."

''GERB," I shouted into the phone. "It's Jerry. Janssen left. He got in his limo and he's gone."

Silence.

"Can you fix the scene, Jerry?" a subdued Gerber asked.

"Yeah, I'll figure something out," I told him, mentally resigning myself to the enormous added pressure of chopping up the script, getting the lines sorted and redistributed to the other actors, and trying to make the scene work—with the clock ticking.

I managed to pull it off except for a close-up we shot later, but not without an unjustifiable burden placed upon all involved.

It was already hard enough to work around David's ever-increasing surliness, but there was just nothing excusable about leaving the set in the middle of a scene. I never quite forgave Janssen for that one.

As it turned out, I had company.

A ritual is performed on every set at the completion of each actor's run on a show. There is a pause in the work, and an announcement is made that goes something along the lines of, "Hey, everyone. This a wrap for so-and-so. Everybody say goodbye." This ritual gives the cast and crew the opportunity to extend their good wishes, say their thank-yous, and bid farewell.

When that day arrived for David and the customary announcement was made, Mr. Janssen simply turned his back to the quiet set and walked away, without uttering a single word to anybody. When the big studio door *thunked* shut behind him, the entire crew broke into applause. They were that happy to see him go.

I have never witnessed anything like it before or since.

In spite of the misery he had caused me as a director, I actually felt sadness that day, watching a man of such stellar talent descend into the darkness of professional contempt.

A bright spot on that production, however, was the producer I mentioned before, David Gerber.

A former agent, David was blessed with the gift of gab, and was such a charismatic and persuasive fellow that he made it hard to say no when he wanted you to do something. He may not have had much luck persuading David Janssen that night, but others—such as yours truly—fell under his potent powers of persuasion easily.

It was later that year I that found myself in Toronto in the dead of winter, freezing my ass off while shooting a pilot called *World of Darkness*, when David Gerber called wanting me to do another pilot.

I told him I was just too exhausted to take on another project at the moment, and that I'd have to pass.

Naturally, David insisted and sent the script up to Canada anyway. I agreed to read it, in the hopes of politely ending the discussion.

Never one to turn down a fantastic story, I reasoned that if the script was a gem, then, tired or not, I might consider doing it. Unfortunately, *Cover Girls* was about a bunch of undercover cops posing as sexy models, and the script was dismal at best. Even a story about hot, scantily clad models could do nothing to take the chill out of my bones, the script was so bad.

Remember, I really respected David Gerber. Not wanting to lay out the true reason for my refusal, I didn't call him when I got home to L.A. I hoped the conversation would be forgotten.

"Hey, you're back! Why didn't you call me?" came his chirpy voice on my home phone.

"Yeah, hey, David. I just got back in town. Look, I can't do it. I'm way too tired, and I just cannot do it." I stuck with the "too tired" story to avoid telling him how badly the script sucked.

"Aww, c'mon Jer," he pressed. "You do great work. You have to come in and talk to me. Maybe we'll do some other stuff, too. You've *got* to come see me."

Not wanting to alienate the guy, I agreed to a quick meeting the next day. I knew the meeting wouldn't take long, because I was *not* doing that piece of junk.

I was right, it didn't take long. Not twenty minutes passed before I walked out of his office, after having agreed to do that piece of junk.

Yes, I shot it, and guess what I got? A piece of junk.

Factor in a lead actress sleeping with a co-producer and it all boiled down to a jolly good time.

Not.

Anyway, back to the *World of Darkness* set in Toronto. We had a rather eclectic cast for that pilot, which included Academy Award-winning Beatrice Straight, Sonny van Dusen, who became a lifelong friend, and Tovah Feldshuh, who had the peculiar habit of eating bagels from the center hole out.

Don't ask.

One night I found myself at dinner in a very upscale restaurant with the film's executive producer, David Susskind, and his lovely producer,

Diana Kerew. Susskind, in his arrogant, pompous way, decided to chew on Diana that night instead of the rack of lamb sitting in front of him. On and on he went about what a worthless, know-nothing, poor excuse of a producer she was, with only brief interruptions to toss back his full head of white hair.

Completely mortified by his incessant berating of this poor creature, I kept my head buried in my plate throughout the dinner, struggling to focus on anything other than the perverse humiliation taking place before me.

Relieved when at long last the check arrived, indicating that the night was finally coming to a merciful end, Diana and I follow Susskind— who of course led—out of the restaurant and into the frosty snow-packed night. David, a diminutive guy, misjudging a snowbank by several feet, took one step from the walkway to his waiting taxi and promptly vanished! All that was visible above the drift of snow was his perfect nary-a-hair-out-of-place white head!

Having never seen karma work quite so quickly before, Diana and I darted around the corner of the building, laughing so hysterically that I needed the wall to hold me up!

MORE LIKE MAXI-SERIES

Movies on television proved so popular that just making more of them wasn't enough. How could it be when there was so much great material out there? Countless, inspiring stories of courage and grace born out of tragedy. Historical accounts of greed, deceit, and betrayal, as well as fanciful tales of humor, romance, and joy. Scripts just kept getting better and better. Television movies quickly morphed into longer, richer tales, requiring more time to tell them. Thus, the miniseries was born.

Wheels

Based on an Arthur Hailey book about the automotive industry, *Wheels* was my first miniseries. It was amazing to work with such outstanding performers as Rock Hudson, Lee Remick, Ralph Bellamy, and Tony Franciosa. The level of talent I had been collaborating with was extraordinary and this, my first cast in my first miniseries, was no exception.

Well . . . maybe just one exception.

Lee Remick's work was so fantastic, I felt I owed her an explanation for simply leaving her alone. I called her aside on the set one day just to explain that I didn't ever say much to her because her takes were all perfect. She thanked me, then quietly went on to win an Emmy for her performance.

Rock Hudson had the rather unconventional hobby of needlepoint, and passed time on the set working on his pillow projects. The man was terrific to work with, and extremely supportive of the other actors.

Which brings us to the "one exception."

Hyper, edgy, and high-strung, Tony Franciosa rarely knew his lines, so cue cards were often close at hand. Tension was omnipresent when he was on set.

One night we were shooting a scene with Tony and Rock in a car in the rain, with about eight or nine pages still left to get through. With windshield wipers cued and film rolling, I suddenly heard, "Cut! Cut! CUT!" coming from inside the car.

I walked over to the car to see what was the matter.

"I can't see my cue cards through all this rain!" Tony huffed.

Okaaaay.

The solution ended up being that little tiny cue cards were drawn up and crammed into a small car with the six-foot five-inch Rock Hudson who, in a gesture above and beyond the call of duty, held and managed the mini-cue cards on his chest so Tony could deliver his lines. That's the kind of guy Hudson was.

Jerry and Rock Hudson—*Wheels*

One day as everyone toiled away, we were treated to the umpteenth Franciosa meltdown as Tony suddenly broke character right in the middle of a take. "This is ridiculous!" he shouted, launching into yet another bombastic tirade. "I can't do this many pages in one day!" On and on he went. "There's no way I can do this! I shouldn't have to be put through this."

Everyone's nerves had been worn thin with this behavior. With daggers starting to form in the eyes of the stone-faced crew, I knew I had better step in and do something.

"Tony, Tony, hold on!" I cooed in my most soothing voice. "There's no pressure here. Just relax. We have all the time in the world."

The expressions on the faces of the crew went from icy disdain to shocked bewilderment.

"Why don't you go outside and take a walk," I calmly continued. "Get some fresh air. There's no rush. Just come on back when you're ready."

With the entire set stunned into silence and looking at me like I'd lost my mind, you could have heard a pin drop as I turned and walked back over to my director's chair. Taking a deep breath, I lifted the chair up over my head and hurled it onto the concrete floor, smashing it into bits. Then I jumped on top of it and stomped it into a million pieces!

Yes, even level-headed, problem-solving, even-tempered directors have their limits. I had to release the tension that had been building and building, and the poor chair was the recipient of my pent-up frustration.

After a lengthy pause to process the shock, the entire set busted up laughing. Tony included.

Interestingly, it was much smoother sailing after that.

Tony's temper was no secret in Hollywood. Like so many other souls trying to juggle the double-edged sword of fame and its trappings, Tony had resorted to darker methods of coping with it all.

He smoked. A lot. But what I thought was a serious nicotine addiction turned out to be something much more sinister.

Each time he put a cigarette into his mouth, he would lick the tip of his little finger to wet it, then reach down into his coat pocket for a match. As the match went up to light his cigarette, the finger went up to his nose.

Hyperactive emotional outbursts explained.

It took me awhile to catch on, but eventually I spotted the routine.

Sadly, I would go on to witness the high cost many enormously gifted people paid for substance abuse.

That Wasn't in the Script!

Evening in Byzantium

I was thrilled when the quantity and quality of projects heading my way began to rival anything I'd seen on the big screen.

Based on the novel by Irwin Shaw, *Evening in Byzantium* was a saga eerily ahead of its time about terrorists overtaking the Cannes Film Festival in France. It was another four-hour miniseries starring Glenn Ford, Eddie Albert, Erin Grey, and Shirley Jones, with whom I'm always delighted to work. It had a fabulous cast, but the script was weak. The producer promised me a rewrite AND a trip to Cannes to shoot a good portion of the movie, both of which worked toward overcoming my misgivings about committing to the project. Let's face it, a few weeks in the south of France can go a long way toward placating one's reservations.

Weeks of prep went by and still no rewrite, so I went ahead and started shooting the parts of the script that I could do in Los Angeles.

One scene took place on a yacht out in the L.A. harbor. Didn't get lucky with Mother Nature that day; the weather was unusually rough. The cast and crew—including yours truly— got tossed around pretty good, to the point that we all ending up spewing over the side of the boat. Nevertheless, the tossing of cookies and the misery it entailed wasn't going to prevent me from getting the shots.

Thinking on my feet—or in this case on my knees—I knew I had to pick my green ass up off the deck and keep going. I finally decided to move the boat just inside the breakwater and position cameras out away from shore. Shot safely from the barf-free zone, the shots looked as if we were way out at sea.

Working with Glenn Ford proved to be a serious challenge, as well. It was no secret in Hollywood that he liked his martinis. As long as cue cards were present at every take—and more importantly as long as you got his scenes done before noon—it was doable.

Unfortunately, I had to find out that last part the hard way.

We were shooting an intense scene between Glenn and Erin Grey, a new actress in her first role who was playing his daughter. A furious argument between the characters required him to slap Erin in the heat of the moment. Regrettably, the scene was scheduled right after lunch. Glenn's lunch having apparently been mostly liquid resulted in him landing a solid blow square to Erin's face. He hit her so hard, the impact knocked her to the ground! To say she was upset would be a colossal understatement, but she pulled herself together and carried on like a pro.

After a couple of weeks of shooting, I was still waiting for the new pages to arrive. Time was running out. With me retching my guts out on a boat and my wife at home practicing her French, this trip to Cannes was more needed than ever, so I decided to make my way in to see the producer. I wanted answers to two questions: When are we getting the new script, and when are we heading to Cannes?

"Don't worry Jerry. The new pages are coming," he assured me. "Oh, but I've got some bad news," he said, clearing his throat before dropping the bomb. "You have to stay here to film the L.A. stuff, so you're going to miss Cannes."

"So who's gonna shoot it?" I asked, thrown by this bit of news and just a tad more than miffed.

"I'm sending my production guy. Give him a list of the shots you need, huh?" He zipped out the door before I could respond.

No trip to the south of France and no rewrite ever materialized.

Oh, did I forget to mention the producer's name was Glen Larsen?

After editing my cut here in L.A., I contacted Mr. Larsen, who happened to be in Hawaii, to tell him I'd finished and the director's cut was ready for his review.

"Oh, hey, Jerry. I won't be home for another two weeks," he said. "Why don't you bring the film and your wife to Hawaii and we can run it here?"

Yeah, and I've got some swampland in Florida . . .

Still, when does Hawaii NOT sound like a good idea? That, and having been burned on the French Riviera shoot, I agreed to take Glen up on his offer, half-wondering if the trip would actually materialize. This time Glen stayed true to his word. Two tickets for a week in Hawaii arrived for me and Marilynn. So, with film in tow, off to Oahu we went.

While I had issues with many other facets of Glen Larsen, he was actually a very accommodating host. He took us to see various sights and shows. Each night we enjoyed dinners with our wives. Every day I would ask him if today was a good time to run the film for him. Each day the answer was the same. I was told to "hang in there." He was too busy today, maybe tomorrow.

After a very enjoyable week in Hawaii, Marilynn and I boarded a jet home to L.A. with the unopened film canister. Glen never viewed a single frame.

Not long after that shoot, I got a call from another producer inquiring about how things went with Glenn Ford on *Evening in Byzantium.* Not wanting to say anything disparaging about an old Hollywood legend, I paused. "What kind of movie are you doing?" I asked, choosing my words carefully.

"We're doing a western. What do you think?"

"Well, do you have a horse that can carry cue cards?" I said, trying to lightly dodge a potentially heavy conversation.

"Oh, cue cards. Okay. Thank you very much," he said, and that was the end of the conversation.

I got off the phone, frankly quite proud of myself for having managed to avoid maligning a Hollywood icon by not offering up testimony to an obvious drinking problem.

Two nights later, about 5:00 in the evening, my home phone rang.

"Haalllo Jerry. Thith is Glenn Ford," slurred the angry voice at the other end of the line.

"Hi, Glenn. How ya doin'?" *Oh, this is gonna be trouble.*

"Why'd you tell tha' producer I needed cue cards?" he sputtered.

"Well, Glenn, as you may remember, we had cue cards for you in every single scene. I had to be honest with him."

Weeelll . . . yeah I had 'em there, but I never looked at 'em!" he bellowed.

I was speechless.

"Oh, I'm gonna get ya for thith!" With that, he slammed the receiver down.

No matter how honest or even how innocent, never say anything about anybody and assume it won't get back to them.

Goes a long way to explain why so many lies get told in this industry.

Oh, and one more thing. . . . Glenn got hired for that western anyway. Must have found that cue card-carrying horse!

PATTY DUKE—A REAL MIRACLE WORKER

With the miniseries format really catching fire, drawing bigger and better talent and scripts, I found myself going right from one movie to another.

Women in White was a four-hour miniseries for NBC. A medical drama shot in Miami, it had a fantastic cast starring Academy Award winner Patty Duke.

She was a magnificent actress, and her mastery in front of the camera was never more evident than in one particular scene where she had no dialogue at all. It was an intense scene where her character, a nurse, was at her terminally ill father's bedside to euthanize him. Patty never uttered a single word during that lengthy take, but when she had finished, every single person on the set was in tears. She was beyond brilliant.

My job by definition is to get the very best I can—from actors, locations, lighting, sets, costumes—down on film. However, it's an entirely different experience to witness some of the most moving performances for film, live and up close. You never quite know when these bolts of soul-stirring moments will occur, but when they do, everyone feels it. They are spellbinding flashes captured in the heart and frozen in the mind as well as on film. That scene with Patty Duke was one of them. It's the most cherished aspect of my job by far.

One night on *Women in White*, we were shooting a party scene on the rooftop of a hospital. It was a Halloween party and the set looked great: spooky decorations all over the place, beer kegs everywhere, and sixty extras decked out in costumes of every imagining. Miami being Miami, it started to rain pretty hard shortly after we began shooting, so we had to stop and wait about an hour or so for the storm to pass. Of course, we kept everyone on standby so we could resume filming as soon as the rain let up.

What I didn't know was that the beer kegs on the set were full of real beer. By the time we started rolling again, the extras were a quite a rambunctious, rollicking bunch, all wasted out of their minds!

Best party scene I ever filmed!

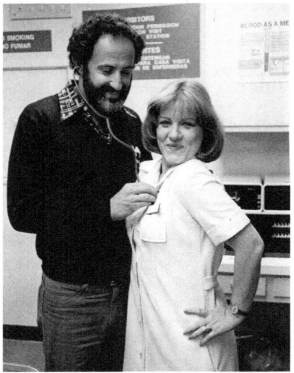

Jerry and Patty Duke

Konichiwa—The Adventure of a Lifetime

B y this point in time, the miniseries format was moving at a frenzied pace. Networks were scrambling to beat each other to the top of the ratings pyramid. To get the next big property (that would be the chatter on everyone's lips at the water coolers in every office building in America) was every major studio's objective, and competition was fierce.

Television was more powerful and influential during that period than it had ever been. This was the time when gripping stories like *Roots*, *Rich Man, Poor Man*, and *Shōgun* would totally eclipse the power and influence of the feature film industry.

Think about it. Most feature films tell their stories in about two hours. Sometimes less. The unprecedented film classic, *Gone with the Wind*, was considered a behemoth at four hours!

The television miniseries format had the enormous advantage of taking six, eight, even upwards of twelve hours for a story to build and climax.

We had the very best Emmy and Academy Award-winning set decorators, costume designers, special effects, locations, production staffs, and talent that existed in the industry. With the incredible luxury of time, talent, and production values to match, we were endowed with the ability to engage and enrapture a television audiences like nothing before ever had.

Why?

There are several reasons. The days of DVR systems at home were still a long way off; Betamax tapes were just beginning to appear, and they were as about as sophisticated as it got. In those days, if something aired and you missed it . . . too bad. You couldn't just press a button to record a popular show when you weren't home and watch it later. It was called a rerun and you had wait for it, usually for several months.

There was a mass collective experiential energy that took place when these stories were televised because everyone watched at exactly the same time and nobody wanted to be excluded from the conversation.

The spectrum of influence was enormous. Shrewd advertisers knew it, and budgets swelled accordingly.

Roots singlehandedly proved to nervous network executives, who kept insisting that mainstream America would not tune in to watch black heroes and heroines, that they were dead wrong. *Roots* paved the way for a proliferation of positive black character-driven TV programming.

With America collectively captivated, toilets all over the country flushed at the same time, meaning no one was watching the commercials. When movie theaters sat empty night after night, theater owners simply closed.

Television was a very different creature back then.

My hard work on episodic television during those years earned me a reputation as a consistent, reliable director who got big production values, even with small budgets. I believe that's what induced Paramount to come calling when they obtained the rights to James Clavell's runaway bestselling novel, *Shōgun*.

I remembered the comments my wife Marilynn, an avid reader, had made when she finished reading the novel months prior. "This is an absolutely fantastic story," she said, tossing the book onto a table, "but they'll never be able to get it all into a movie. It would be impossible to tell this tale in a couple of hours."

But I didn't hear the thud of a book hitting the table that day. Nope. What I heard was the thud of a gauntlet being thrown down. I've always loved a challenge and the accompanying adrenaline rush of thinking on my feet. In my mind, just hearing the words, "It can't be done," was a call to arms. Well, maybe not in two hours, but . . .

Paramount knew I had already directed three miniseries, so they were staunchly behind me in taking the helm of this massive, twelve-hour project. However, there was one catch. James Clavell himself had to approve me.

And his word was final.

By this time, I had read the book and I badly wanted it.

Needless to say, I could not wait for the phone to ring following the big powwow with Paramount, NBC, and Mr. Clavell to find out whether or not I had been approved. Actors aren't the only ones tortured by the "audition" process.

The long-anticipated call came. After the champagne was popped and congratulatory slaps on the back subsided, the sobering reality of the enormity of this twelve-hour project began to set in. That buzz of euphoria wore off pretty quickly when I read the first page of the script, which was entitled, "Storm at Sea." During my shoot on *Evening in Byzantium*, I had colorfully proven that I'd been born without "sea legs."

Nevertheless, the first order of business was to meet with the Emmy Award-winning scriptwriter Eric Bercovici. We made arrangements for the introduction to take place at his home in Beverly Hills. I liked Eric instantly. The twinkle in his eye betrayed his wicked sense of humor.

I would soon learn to value his honesty, as well.

"Do you realize what you're getting into, Jerry?" he asked, leaning one arm over the typewriter on his brightly lit desk.

"What do you mean?" I asked with a blank stare.

"Your whole life is going to be uprooted," he said, peering straight into my eyes. "You're going to be in Japan for an entire year, and you'll spend at least another year in post at Paramount."

He wasn't finished. "What will this do to your family? Do you really want to sacrifice two years of your life for this?"

To be honest, I had been so engrossed in the magnitude of the storytelling that I hadn't spent much time focusing on the personal impact the project would make on my life.

I would be the first director ever at the helm of every episode in this long-form miniseries format. *Roots* had had four different directors, one for each of its four episodes. I would be directing all five episodes of *Shōgun*.

The impact a year's absence would have on my family would be significant. My daughter Lisa was just starting college, but my son Todd was still at home in high school.

After the initial shock wore off, Marilynn and I made plans. We would bring the kids to Japan for the entire summer, and Marilynn would make as many trips back and forth as she could in order to keep connected in both worlds.

No one ever said this kind of life was easy, especially on families. Hollywood exceeds the averages in divorce rates, as the strain of filmmaking is felt throughout the families.

We moved into preproduction. As the vast majority of the characters were either British or Japanese, I immediately found myself onboard a jet for England to begin casting alongside James Clavell, who resided in London, and casting director Maude Specter, who had cast the monumental film, *Lawrence of Arabia*, as well as many of the classic *James Bond 007* films.

I have had spectacular luck with unearthing tremendous talent in England. Finding and casting John Rhys-Davies at the onset of his career for this project was no exception.

Then it was straight to Japan to cast the Japanese roles, as well as get on with the scouting of countless locations.

And I *do* mean countless.

With one thousand and sixty-two scenes in a script filled with sea battles, earthquakes, and ninja attacks, let me assure you this was no small endeavor.

Neither were casting and hiring an almost exclusively Japanese-speaking cast and crew, with communication funneled through interpreters. In fact, because so few Japanese people spoke English at that time, just about everything in all departments was done through interpreters.

While offers for the lead were going out to several high-profile actors like Sean Connery and Albert Finney, we were thrilled when we got word that Richard Chamberlain had accepted the lead role of Anjin-san/Major Blackthorne. Having long admired his work, I knew he'd be perfect in the role.

We were allotted a twelve-million-dollar budget, a hefty sum in those days. But with numerous epic battle scenes, 100% foreign and often very remote locations, and the size of the storyboard (which filled an entire room top to bottom), it soon became obvious to everyone involved that it would be impossible to accomplish this herculean project on twelve-million-dollars. Every aspect of *Shōgun* was to be of superior quality, right down to the painstakingly hand-crafted kimonos and hand-painted sets.

The first solution to this predicament was that James Clavell instructed Eric to go in and trim down the battle scenes in the script (which he did—about forty pages' worth) without losing any of the story. This move alone saved us a chunk of change right up front, but it still wasn't enough.

Lucky for us, Clavell was not only committed and determined to see his book on film, he was also well connected. He went to his high-level contacts in Hong Kong and sold the distribution rights for another three million. He then went to back to NBC and to TV Asahi, the Japanese network, and raised millions more, bringing the total to eighteen million dollars. At the end of the day, with postproduction publicity, etc., and a brilliant musical score by Maurice Jarre, who scored *Lawrence of Arabia* and *Dr. Zhivago*, *Shōgun* ended up being a twenty-million-dollar production, a colossal budget for television in those days.

And that was 1979 money!

With preproduction well underway, locations set, and casting partially complete, three months had already passed. I returned home to collect more clothes and say goodbye to my family. Then I picked up what was ready of the script and headed back to Japan to set up base camp in what would be my "home" for the rest of the year.

Nothing could have prepared me for what awaited.

My Blood Brother

I was ready for the fact that cultural differences would naturally present some challenges—surely nothing insurmountable—but there was far more in store that would provoke disconnect between our cultures than the unfamiliar concept of eating raw fish. I would soon learn that even the exacting aspects of filmmaking were not immune to the cultural divide and the accompanying frustration it created.

Some I could anticipate. Some I could not.

"Eric, I need you here in Japan," I said, hoping the long-distance echo would mask the desperation in my voice.

"I don't know if I'd be any help, Jerry," he replied. "Besides, I've still got to get the script finished."

This was not going to be an easy sell, but I knew when I first met him that Eric was a straight-up, trustworthy guy with a great sense of humor, qualities that would be very helpful in co-piloting this journey.

I reasoned that without Clavell present and no producer on set to help sort through the ever-mounting obstacles, who better than the scriptwriter to help me navigate and adjust complex scenes on the fly? In fact, Eric should be the producer. I succeeded in getting his attention, but still no commitment.

"I need an ally here, Eric. It's gonna be a war, just like you predicted."

"Okay, Jer, if Paramount agrees, I'll make the trip down, but I'm not committing myself to anything beyond assessing the situation," he warned.

That was good enough for me. I needed a partner and a confidante, and I knew I'd have one when he stepped off the plane into this Pandora's box of a shoot. At least, that's what I was counting on.

With Paramount's blessing, Eric was on the next plane to Tokyo.

He never left my side the rest of the entire shoot. Eric was that kind of guy.

Eric Bercovici, my partner

On and off the set, his help was immeasurable. We worked in tandem, modifying the complications of scenes and locations. All the while, he simultaneously finished writing the script.

He was supportive beyond words. He was my sounding board, and my "fix-it guy" when things got out of hand.

We are lucky if we find even one person on this journey through life who has our back the way Eric had mine, so it's not surprising that a lifelong friendship was formed as a result of this arduous and grueling journey together.

I'LL HAVE WHAT HE'S HAVING

I always welcome opportunities to build rapport with my actors. Shortly after Eric arrived, we were delighted to accept a dinner invitation to meet our Japanese lead in the role of Lord Yoshi Toranaga. It seems Mr. Toshiro Mifune, the most famous Japanese actor of all time, wanted to get to know the *gaijin* (foreigners) he would be working with over the next year.

No expense or effort was spared in presenting the finer points of Japanese culinary culture that night. The dinner was prepared by Tokyo's finest master chef.

Sake was consumed like water. It wasn't long before Eric and I realized that, much like the machismo of rounds of shots in a bar back home or perhaps pints of Guinness flowing in an Irish pub, the ability to consume mass quantities of sake was a bit of Japan's masculine bravado posturing.

Jerry, Toshiro Mifune, and Eric

Now, except for the occasional well-aged scotch, I'm not much of a drinker. But the steely gleam in Eric's eye that night told me he was intent on doing his best to hang in with this showdown. As the toast, *Kanpai*, ("dry the glass") got more and more frequent, I watched Eric get shorter and shorter in his seat. Concluding that it would be wholly disloyal—even slightly treasonous—to let him go it alone, I did my best to keep up with our foreign hosts.

I don't really remember all that much about that night, but when I could resume speech late the next day I was told that it had been a delicious dinner and that I'd had a very good time!

FINDING MY WEI

There were only thirty Americans in a one-hundred-and-fifty-person crew, making the vast majority Japanese nationals, so *all* departments were operated through interpreters, mostly female.

In efforts to manage communications, a day typically started with me gathering the entire crew on the set and giving my outlines and instructions to my interpreter, a lovely lady named Wei, who would then turn to the crew and translate what I had said. They would ask questions and she would come back to me, translating their inquiries. I would clarify the questions and she would address the crew again in Japanese, translating my answers. This process went on for about fifteen minutes for every single setup, every single day. By the end of the first week I was one entire day behind schedule. Do the math—on a twenty-six-week shoot, that's going to be a massive setback!

I thought about this problem all through the weekend, struggling to come up with a solution.

When I got back to work on Monday morning, I called Wei over to share with her the only idea I had come up with. "Okay," I said, "we've gotta do something different, because we are just burning up too much time. So, we're gonna give this a try. When we get the crew together each morning, I'm going to speak directly to them and see if that works." I paused, looking for her reaction.

"They will not understand what you are telling them," she said.

"I don't care. I'll speak loud!" I blurted as I hurried over to my chair. A nonsensical assertion at best. But I was afraid she might be right.

When everyone gathered for the morning instructions, I went directly to the front and began issuing my dictates and plans for the day in English. Then I turned and walked back to my chair, irrationally hoping for the best. The crew approached Wei for clarification in Japanese, which she provided. Then everyone went about the business of getting on with the day.

Wow. That actually worked.

Having successfully streamlined communication by brilliantly eliminating two steps in the process, by the end of that week we were back on schedule. I was very proud of myself. In fact, my arms grew a little longer from patting myself on the back!

Shōgun—Wei, interpreter

"I got word that Paramount is very happy we're back on schedule," I boasted to Wei at lunch a few days later. "Good thing I came up with that idea to talk to the crew directly."

"Yes, that is good news. But that was not the reason," she replied.

"What do you mean?" I asked indignantly.

"In Japan, they do not like to take orders from a woman. It is because you stopped speaking to me first that they started to listen to you," she said stoically. "They will cooperate if you speak to them before you speak to me. That is just the way things are in Japan." With that, she went back to eating her calamari.

So even though they hadn't understood a word I said, the fact that I addressed them before I spoke to my highly competent interpreter—who just happened to be female and who would have to interpret what I said anyway—put things right in their minds, so they could get on with work.

Japan was still such a patriarchal society at that time that women walked behind their men on the streets!

While at this point I shouldn't have been surprised, the cultural gender divide hardly ended there.

As we began shooting scenes with the Japanese actresses playing geisha, I started to notice that whenever I would step in front of the girls to direct a scene, no one would look at me; they looked down as soon as I began to speak. I was baffled by this shy behavior. These *were* actresses, after all.

With a scene coming up that included Major Blackthorn receiving a very friendly massage from several giggly geisha offering, shall we say, "less than shy behavior," averting one's eyes was not the energy I was looking for. Yet Japanese culture at that time dictated that women should avert their eyes out of respect when being addressed by a man.

Sometimes it felt like the year 1665, even when the cameras *weren't* rolling.

Having never harbored any desire for a Screen Actor's Guild card, I wasn't about to 'act out' what I needed from these actresses, so I enlisted my steadfast Wei to offer some guidance with this latest predicament in communication. Her solution was for me to speak a few words to the girls in Japanese, so she came up with a couple of simple phrases she thought might help get their attention—and more importantly, their eyes—on me.

We first tried, *"Anata no hada wa raisupēpā hodo yawarakai,"* which basically translates to: You have skin as soft as rice-paper—a serious form of flattery in that culture. When that failed to get the response I needed, the ever-practical and no-nonsense Wei surprised me with this one: *"Anata wa kawaii oshiri wo motte imasu.* Loosely translated: You have a cute butt.

Apparently that one gets attention in any language, because it sure did the trick! In fact, after that, they never stopped staring at me, probably wondering what the hell I would say next!

On master shots, I'd shoot the sequence with two or three cameras, then take a pause to confer with my director of photography and first assistant director before moving on to the close-up shots, only to turn around and find the Japanese crew tearing down the whole scene.

Close-ups? What close-ups??

81

A geisha

If you take a look at the works of legendary Japanese director Akira Kurosawa, very seldom will you ever see a close-up; everything was done in one shot. So the crew just assumed that when the master shot was done, the scene was done.

No history with it. Okay, I can understand that to a point, but this went on for weeks. It was as if the last time I asked them to leave the set alone and move on to close-ups was the last time I was *ever* going to ask them to leave the set alone and move on to close-ups! It didn't seem to sink in that it was a standing order. The constant vigilance was draining.

The camera cranes at our disposal were of the antiquated teeter-totter style, with the operator balanced—or not—at one end, which made for some pretty static shots. Fortunately, I brought my favorite camera operator Chuy Elizondo from the states to help instruct the Japanese crew on how to get the most from the dated gear.

Even the simple process of booking an actor for a job was problematic. When you book an American actor, you contract them for the duration of a role, so should the shooting schedule require a change, no big deal. In the Japanese system, you booked only by the day(s), so should the shooting schedule change, chaos ensued. Of course, you'd never get through a production of this magnitude without running up against unexpected adjustments, so I was repeatedly forced to juggle, cut, and rearrange the shooting schedule.

The energy spent in continual pleas for an essential prop or even something as easy as ice for my drinks made getting my job done a frustrating, unnecessary headache. It amounted to a constant grind, which sapped the resolve of many to see this through to the end.

After nearly four weeks of shooting, my first assistant director, with whom I had worked on many shows at Universal and had hand-picked to come with me from the States, finally gave up and quit. He told me he just couldn't hack it anymore, and flew back to LA. He was followed shortly thereafter by my American prop man.

As more key members of the sparse American crew quit, and more and more seemingly insurmountable complications accumulated, my own level of resilience began to fade. My wife's words of warning that *Shōgun* would be "impossible" began to haunt me.

The echoes of Eric's questioning on the first day we met, *"You wanna sacrifice two years of your life for this?"* had me contemplating booking my own flight out of there. Maybe the project really wasn't worth it, after all.

After an exhausting week of shooting, I would spend every Saturday in the editing room. By the time the fourth Saturday rolled around, I found I could barely muster enough enthusiasm to go in. Forcing down yet another bowl of rice gave me just enough thrust to at least head out the door that morning.

Everything changed for me when I looked over my rough cut of the first hour. I knew I had something very special on my hands. A once-in-a-career-if-you're-lucky kind of special. The mystical beauty that jumped off the film that day gave me the determination I needed to stick it out.

I just had to find a way to withstand the relentless obstacles.

THE MARIKO MARATHON

Adding to the frustrations, the lead actress in the role of Mariko quit just before filming started. Seems the concept of her being hired for the full six months had been lost on her manager. Upon looking over her shoot schedule, he checked off countless dates she wasn't available because of a concert tour she had scheduled during the entire six-month shoot!

We hastily rearranged our shoot schedule as best we could to shoot around Mariko's scenes in order to buy more time to find another actress. Casting worked as quickly as they could with nights and weekends, spending every spare moment interviewing Japanese actresses—to no avail. It was incredibly difficult to find a girl who could speak coherent English.

With weeks rapidly passing and no suitable candidates on the horizon, we were desperate for a solution. Paramount came up with the brilliant idea of hiring an English or American actress and putting her in "Japanese makeup."

Japanese makeup??

That's when Eric and I put our collective foot down. Make that move and we are both *out*.

So the search for a Japanese Mariko continued.

One Saturday, as Eric and I endured yet another myriad of actresses grinding through a reading in unintelligible English, we indifferently busied ourselves at the table, with neither of us even looking at the stage. Suddenly, over the paper shuffling, we heard a sweet voice speaking English that we could actually understand. Both of our heads snapped in the direction of the stage. Eric and I could scarcely believe what we were seeing—a petite beauty giving a damned good reading in clear English! We were so shocked, we asked her to repeat the scene.

Just five days before we had to shoot Mariko's first scene, at long last we had found our star! Yoko Shimada was the perfect Mariko. Ecstatic, we scrambled to our feet to hastily introduce ourselves, then quickly

85

whispered to the Japanese casting people, "Do *not* let her out of the building until she signs a contract!"

Yoko Shimada—Mariko

STOP BUGGING ME

Having completed what we could on sound stages in Tokyo, the next part of the shoot moved us out of the urban and on to a location in more rural environs to create the set town of Anjiro.

Much more rural.

As in primitive sixteenth century feudal Japan rural. So remote and so isolated was this minute cove near Nagashima that no road into this tiny fishing village even existed! A road actually had to be created. That's right. Even trees had to be removed to create a road just to get us and our gear there. (The trees had to be replaced upon our departure.)

We were presented with two options for accommodations during our six-week shoot in the tiny village. The first was a room at the single hotel in town, which had been closed down for years but was being taken over and revamped by the production staff. The second was lodging at an existing hotel an hour's drive away. Given that the shooting schedules for this segment of the film were mostly at night—approximately 5:00 p.m. to 5:00 a.m.—I decided another two hours in a car each day was too big a price to pay, so I took a room at the village "hotel."

When I showed up to check in, I was informed that the full staff had not yet arrived to complete the refurbishment. A room was nevertheless ready for me. After a quick glance around the room, I called my wife, who was still in Tokyo, and asked her to bring soap and towels when she made the trip down a few days later.

Not exactly five star, but . . . oh, who am I kidding? It made a Motel 6 look like The Ritz. But what the heck—the only time I was going to be in the room was to sleep. Right? So I checked into my cramped quarters to get some much-needed rest before the start of shooting the following day.

Sometime during the night, I woke up to use the bathroom and flipped the switch on a little lamp that was precariously balanced on my tiny nightstand. There on the ceiling was the weirdest, most massive crablike beetle creature I had ever not wanted to see in my entire lifetime!! This thing was the size of a small shoe, with spindly legs sticking out everywhere!

Arming myself with my boot and a towel, I managed to knock the thing down from the ceiling, throw the towel over it, and proceed to beat the hell out of it!

Director -1.

Spine-chilling Insect - 0.

With that little drama behind me, I settled back in the bed in futile pursuit of the sleep I desperately needed if I wanted to be sharp the next day. After tossing and turning for an hour, I gave up and turned the light on again, maybe to read or something. It was a move that set off what sounded like the rustling of thousands of crusty feet scurrying to find cover.

Spine-chilling Insects - 1000.

Director - Outta there.

I grabbed my luggage with lightning speed, and headed for the door, trying hard to push from my mind the thought that any of the little buggers might have sought shelter inside my bags.

The best I could do at 3:00 a.m. was the couch in the lobby; I half-expected I might have to fight off one of the wild monkeys in the trees just outside the hotel door for it.

I must have dozed off for a while before the Japanese hotel staff found me at 6:30 the next morning.

In spite of repeated assurances from the staff that the bug problem would be cleaned up, I had already concluded that, in the face of sleeping in a room that was an entomologist's wet dream, the two hours of driving each day probably wasn't so awful after all. I would be moving to the established hotel out of town, and that was the end of that.

Allow me to take a moment to define the word "established" when referring the new hotel. Established, yes, but in traditional Japanese hotel style. There were a whopping four "Western" rooms, meaning tiny rooms with actual beds off the floor. The rest were furnished with tatami mats directly on the floor. There were no laundry facilities, so if you wanted clean anything, you had to wash it by hand in the bathroom sink. It seemed the ritual of cooking a whole fish in one's room was customary, as every morning the hallway was littered with fish carcasses outside the door of almost every room.

The scent of a rose garden it was not. It would be several years after I got home before I could eat fish again.

In retrospect, my decision to change hotels had been a good one. Cursory research revealed that my repulsive roommates were likely *gejigeji*, a nightmarish household centipede with fifteen pairs of legs that jump, are fast as hell, hunt at night, and can sting with venom shot through any one of those thirty legs!

Wish like hell I could say that was my only encounter with strange Japanese vermin. Regrettably, it was not, but at least I managed to move my ass out of harm's way.

Or not. . . .

I felt a new level of exhaustion after that first night shoot in our new location. The winding mountain roads made the ride back to town seem even longer. But with the soft jazz the driver had on the radio, the stress of the insect antics the previous night, and a long night of shooting behind me, my eyelids started getting very heavy. I decided the long drive each night would be a great time to doze off and catch up on some badly needed shuteye.

Unfortunately, so did my driver.

There's just nothing like the thought of plummeting over the edge of a cliff to your spectacular death to snap you right awake! The driver couldn't understand a single word I was saying, so when the car started to wander all over that narrow mountain road, I pounced over the seat to the radio dial to turn the music up. Loud. I tried to sing along, often making up my own lyrics, or chattered on and on about nothing just to keep the guy awake!

This went on every night for six weeks. Moving from a room filled with crab-like bugs to a new location with a sleeping driver was clearly a case of "going from the frying pan into the fire" if ever there was one!

In Nagashima, we were followed everywhere by the town's little children, who stared at us in bewildered fascination. They had never laid eyes on Caucasians before. Relative to what they were used to, we were towering giants, some of us sporting beards, mustaches, and various other facial adornments that were foreign to their eyes, so as far as these kids were concerned, we might as well have been from Mars.

We got used to our little parade of followers and in time became quite friendly with them.

One day as we were making our way through the village, we noticed that our regular group of diminutive sidekicks were otherwise preoccupied on a street corner. They were standing in a large circle shouting and cheering. Curious, we decided to divert slightly off our path to see what the hoopla was about. It appeared they were engaged in a game of racing toy cars or something.

Or something, indeed.

They were racing all right, we had that part right. But not toy cars. What looked like little Hot Wheels from a distance turned out to be their giant six-inch pet cockroaches!

As I stood there grappling with the concept of arthropod as play toy, one of the kids slipped up behind me and put one of the monsters on my shoulder! I'm not sure the high pitch of my "request" to remove the insect was heard all the way to Tokyo, but I wouldn't bet against it!

So abundant were these creatures that the night drives down to the set on the beach at the edge of town sounded like we were driving over Rice Krispies! Snap, crackle, pop throughout the whole drive. While nauseating at the beginning, the sound was so pervasive that after a few weeks I got so used to it that I scarcely noticed it.

Lest you think I was the only one disturbed by the omnipresence of these nasty creatures, I stumbled across written proof that I was not. On my way to use the rather primitive facilities on set one day, I read the following graffiti scribbled on the wall near the latrine: "Do not throw toothpicks into the urinal, as the cockroaches use them to pole vault with."

Enough said.

OUT OF THE FRYING PAN
AND INTO THE SEA

With much of the *Shōgun* story revolving around the sea, a good deal of it had to be shot on the water. In order to get the interior scenes and close-ups of the ships before setting out into the open water, we set up models of the ships on sound stages back in Tokyo. The life-sized mockups were hoisted onto a large raised platform and mounted on a gimbal, which rocked back and forth, simulating the natural movement of a ship a sea.

I quickly discovered that even stepping onto this platform sent my guts into spin cycle, and me into dry heaves.

You heard it here—seasick indoors. Quite a talent, huh?

This didn't bode well for my numerous location shoots on the open water. Attempts to banish into the deep recesses of my mind the dread of the day we must take to the sea didn't help.

It arrived anyway.

I was pacing the dock, trying to psych myself into going aboard, when I was alerted that our fleet of boats—including three for the cameras—was ready to go. Moving to board, I noticed one of the English actors popping a pill.

"What have you got there?" I asked.

"Just the greatest seasick pill ever," he said confidently. "Want one?"

Hearing a much-needed answer to my prayers, I thanked God and the actor, then quickly swallowed what I hoped would be my liberation from intestinal bondage on the high seas.

We got no more than twenty minutes out onto the water before I started to feel that all-too-familiar seasick type of headache. So I headed over to my English friend to ask if his pill seemed to be working for him.

"Fantastic!" was the chipper response. "Brilliant, aren't they?"

"No," I groaned. "Maybe I'd better take another one."

Surprised, he pulled a bottle from his uniformed pocket and handed me another pill.

Just as the anchors dropped and all boats and actors were positioned into place and we prepared to roll on our first shot, I really started to feel the queasiness rising. I dashed over to my English actor buddy, who was at this point my only shot at salvation, to report my worsening condition.

"These pills aren't working," I grumbled. "I'm fading fast here."

"Well, blimey," he said with a blank stare. "I've never heard anybody say they didn't work before."

I'm not sure if my condition embarrassed him or if he was just afraid of having to watch the director launch a Technicolor yawn right in front of him, but he jammed a third pill into my hand. "Here, take another," he said, and dashed off as quickly as he could.

The next thing I remember is being carried off the boat onto the docks. I came to long enough to thrust the days' shot list into Eric's hand, slurring, "Ya gotta these done" before being left on shore to recover for the day.

Guess I should'a asked what was in those pills.

Thanks to the stability of dry land and the drugs slowly fading from my system, by the time I could see the boats returning at the end of the day, I was feeling much better.

I noticed one figure stomping toward me from the docks, wearing a dark scowl. It was Eric.

"Don't ever give me that *Oh, I'm seasick* excuse again, you son-of-a-bitch!" he growled. "You're getting your ass back out there tomorrow! I am *never* working with actors *ever* again!"

I burst into laughter.

Luckily for me, Eric, and pregnant women everywhere, my next day at sea went much better, thanks to another benign little anti-nausea pill called Bonine.

NFW!

Galley slave ship

We were fast approaching what was to be the most challenging scene we had scheduled yet—an epic battle on the water at night. It was a massive undertaking, with twenty small fishing boats loaded with armed Samurai warriors forming a blockade on the water. Blackthorne, on his galley slave ship, was to run through this blockade of fishing boats as they launched an attack on his ship.

Logistics were daunting to say the least, but I love a challenge.

We set up on a jetty at about 4:00 that afternoon, where Eric, my three Japanese ADs, numerous cameramen, and I continued our discussions of the technicalities of getting this sequence down.

Basically, all I needed was for the Samurai fishing boats (each of which was loaded with explosive charges) to get into a straight line. Then, upon my hand signal to Richard Chamberlain who was gallantly perched on the bow of his ship, he would give the verbal cue via a single English word, "Now," to all the Japanese-speaking stuntmen Samurai warriors aboard the fishing vessels below him. They would detonate the charges, blowing their boats to smithereens and, *voilà*, the monumental battle would begin.

I had all three camera boats in the water, one for the master shot and two for opposite views. Eric and I were heading out on a barge to get closer to the action. It was, after all, a one-take deal. Once the boats were blown to bits, that was it.

What could possibly go wrong?

We set up the lighting on the seawall, giving us about a fifty-yard reach out onto the water to light all the boats which, of course, had to stay within that space. Unfortunately, the current kept moving the boats out of line, making it impossible for them to stay in frame for the shot, let alone stay lit.

Seems we should have included Mother Nature in on the meetings for our plans.

After a few hours of watching the boats bob this way and that, I saw my Japanese ADs approaching in unison.

"Mister London-san, we have problem," lamented one of them. "We cannot keep fishing boats lined up in water."

"Well, then try putting anchors on them. Do you have anchors?" I said, thinking I had come up with a fairly simple solution.

The three conferred in Japanese before delivering their predictable refrain. "No, we cannot get anchors."

"Well, then take a rock and tie a line around it or something!" I said, only half-joking.

As the three men wandered off, still sorting through solutions, I heard a snort behind me.

"NFW, Jerry. That's it for tonight. There's just No Fucking Way."

It was Eric.

"No, oh no, no, Eric. I am going to get this shot!" I stated. Undeterred by the setbacks, I headed over to board our small barge to move in a little closer to the action.

"Well, here, then. Take a shot of this," he said, chuckling at my determination. "You're going to need it." He handed me a flask filled with our favorite scotch.

We spent another hour watching boats crisscross in the tide before we heard the call for dinner. Eight o'clock had brought the dinner break and along with it, not a single frame of film shot. Everyone headed back to shore.

"You're never going to get those boats lined up, Jer," Eric said, waving his fork. "It's just not gonna work."

"Aw, c'mon, Eric! Have some faith," I declared, trying to convince myself as well as him. "I can make this happen. You'll see."

After dinner, we set out to the jetty, where lighting was being set in position and cameramen, sound, and dozens of actors were loading into back into the boats. Eric and I boarded our barge, and we all headed back out into the water, just to watch boats ricochet in the tide like rubber ducks in bathtub race.

Glancing at my watch, I saw it was nearly one o'clock in the morning. With dawn arriving in less than three hours that time of year, I thumped Eric. "Gimme that flask, will ya?" I said, in need of a little liquid optimism.

"NFW, Jer," he said with a smirk as he handed over the flask. "NFW."

Realizing I had to do something other than wait for nature's cooperation, I called my ADs over and told them I had a new plan. "We're gonna move the fishing boats about fifty yards farther out and, working with the tide, try to slowly move the galley slave ship instead. Per the original plan, when I feel the timing of tide, boats, and galley are sufficiently lined up, I will give the hand signal to Richard to cue the blasts."

At about 3:30 a.m. we roused everyone from their drowsiness with the new plan, lit the torches, and confirmed the cues. Crossing all my fingers and toes while praying this would actually work, I ordered all cameras to roll.

Sure enough, here came the boats with the tide.

I cued the galley to row. A minute went by as I watched the dozen-plus fishing boats begin to cooperate.

I tossed a triumphant look toward a bemused Eric, who just shook his NFW head.

Another minute passed, and I saw the enormous galley ship drift ever-so-slowly toward its position.

This was gonna work!! I was so excited I could have spit as I watched the tide begin to move the little boats into line. Minutes ticked by like hours as I stood patiently waiting, laser focused and ready to strike, positively *willing* the boats to cooperatively bob into place. Just one more minute and they would all be in a perfect queue. Then we could . . .

"Hey, Jerry!" shouted Richard, shattering the silence across the water from the galleon. "When do I say, 'Now?'"

KABOOOOOM!!!

With that word, everything detonated! Explosions lit up the night sky, stuntmen flew in every direction, the boats exploded into millions of pieces . . . Ten seconds more and the boats would have been in perfect position, but all three cameras just missed getting the shot.

Stunned, I watched the entire scene disintegrate. When I was finally able to raise my jaw up off the floor of the barge to close my mouth, I looked around for Eric, who was nowhere in sight.

Until I looked down.

There he was, rolling on the deck of the barge howling with laughter and waving the flask at me while roaring, "NFW! NFW!"

As the galley slowly drifted by, a mortified Chamberlain looked in my direction. "Guess I fucked up, huh, Jerry?"

Ya think?

No, I couldn't use a single shot from that disastrous operation, and yes, I drained every last drop of scotch in the flask that night!

Two weeks later, with the boats rebuilt, we did the whole thing over again. This time we got the shot!

Jerry the Samurai

Jerry the Shōgun

Director in action

Jerry with Toshiro Mifune

ONION RINGS AND BIG MACS

When Marilynn was with me, she did her very best to alleviate the numbing monotony of eating almost nothing but rice and fish or squid. She employed tactics such as trying to find something resembling chicken at a local market, and simmering it with noodles on a hot plate in our room into something akin to chicken noodle soup. She also brought jars of peanut butter from home. The delight that shot through my bones at the sight of a jar of peanut butter is a true testament to how badly my taste buds had deteriorated.

I wasn't the only one suffering from Western food withdrawal; the steady diet of rice and seafood was wearing thin on everyone. One day on set, word began circulating that we were going to get onion rings for lunch. While onion rings may not have elicited anything more than a grunt back home, this was music to American ears. The chatter about the treat of simple onion rings created a flash mob, with everyone beating a hasty retreat to line up at craft services when the lunch break was called.

The groans of crashing disappointment were audible as we sank our teeth into the "onion rings," only to find we were biting into fried calamari. More squid, only this time in rings! Perhaps to the Americans' deprived palates, that calamari looked enough like onion rings to set off a seismic rumor. Such extended periods of time on a diet so alien to us created what can only be described as a food mirage on the culinary horizon.

After five weeks of this, we were nearing the end of filming in Nagashima. With just one week to go, the production staff brought to my attention that the weather was due to get a bit stormy, and that we might want to consider finishing things up earlier than scheduled, if possible.

They didn't have to ask me twice. There were about two hundred hamburgers with my name on them waiting for me out there somewhere.

I studied the script, and figured out that I could rework a couple of the scenes so we could shoot them in Kyoto, our next stop. All agreed. With the storyboard revised, we managed to cut four whole days off the Nagashima schedule.

We wrapped the last day of shooting on Friday at about 2:00 p.m. I think I was on that bullet train for Kyoto by 2:01 p.m. The crew was to follow the next day.

Safely checked into my two miniscule rooms at the Kyoto Holiday Inn—one just barely fit my luggage, the other just barely fit me—I headed straight for the closest Golden Arches and stuffed myself with hamburgers, fries, and shakes. Cheap, greasy, fried food never tasted so good!!

Saturday came and went, with no sign of the crew. Sunday morning, I heard that a typhoon had hit our little village of Nagashima the night before. Much later, I learned it was Typhoon Tip—the largest typhoon in recorded history—that had hit that side of Japan. The thing was so massive that its diameter could span the distance between Dallas and New York City! Luckily, it had weakened slightly before slamming into the southern shores of Japan, but still it destroyed some twenty thousand homes, with winds strong enough to cause the high-rise buildings in Tokyo to sway.

Every single one of our sets had been completely demolished that night. The village had been devastated, and the train tracks closed. Miraculously, not one of our crew members was hurt. They all managed to make it to Kyoto by Sunday night.

My hat is off to the strength and tenacity of the men and women of our crew. I sure don't know how they did it, but we were up and running by Monday morning.

Never truer were the words, "What a difference a day makes."

SHAKE, RATTLE, AND ROIL

Even fake natural disasters can prove cataclysmic, which was demonstrated by one of our more perilous scenes.

The scene takes places during a dramatic turning point in the story wherein Major Blackthorne once again tries to prove his worthiness to Toranaga, this time by rescuing him from a fissure that swallowed him up during a massive earthquake. A monumental undertaking for filming, indeed.

Not exactly something *Love American Style* had prepared me for.

We found an area outside of Kyoto where heavy rain runoff had carved deep crevices in the ground, some up to twelve feet deep, that resembled earthquake fissures.

Our brilliant special effects guy Bob Dawson created an ingenious system by laying trapdoors over the fissures, which were supported by little wooden arms. He rigged the trapdoors with charges, and then covered them with dirt. When he hit a switch, the charges would detonate and the boards would drop the dirt. Toss in a shaking camera, and boom!!! We would have an earthquake.

Following full days of shooting, we spent every night for the better part of two weeks planning and rehearsing the sequence. With ten cameras set to roll on that day, I was pretty confident we could get it down in one take. Actually, we had no choice—this was another one-take deal.

What could possibly go wrong?

With warriors, horses, background actors, and Chamberlain and Mifune all set and positioned before ten cameras, we were ready to roll.

To ensure the success of this colossal shot, I would begin with the order, "Roll camera one," to which the verbal response from the cameraman would be, "Camera one rolling," and so on down the line with all ten cameras. In spite of the fact that we burned through a good deal of film by the time the word, "Action," echoed over the set, we would second guess nothing to ensure that all ten cameras were functional. We were, after all, doing this once.

"Okay, Bobby. Ready?" I hollered across the set.

"Ready!" he hollered back.

"And . . . ACTION!" I roared.

Bobby hit the switch. Nothing.

"Cut. Reload the cameras," I yelled down the line as I made my way over to my special effects guy.

"What's going on, Bobby?" I asked.

"I don't know, but I'm going to find out," he said, heading for the little entrance to the crevice.

When he reemerged, he reported that the recent rain had turned the loose dirt around the tops of the trapdoors to mud. The mud had dried like cement, so the trapdoors wouldn't release. Fixable, yes, but it would take some time to go around loosening all the dirt and reloading the charges.

Fine. We still had enough daylight to get the shot, so off he went with his crew trailing behind him.

About forty-five minutes later he returned, ready to go. We got everyone in position and began the rolling process again.

"Roll camera one," I shouted.

"Camera one rolling," came the responses all the way down the line to camera ten.

"Okay, Bobby, ready?" I hollered across the set.

"Ready!" he hollered back.

"And . . . ACTION!" I roared.

Again, nothing.

"Cut. Reload the cameras," I yelled out.

"I don't understand this. I can't believe it didn't work!" a puzzled Bobby struggled to explain.

"Bob, I gotta shoot something. With ten cameras rolling, this day is costing big bucks."

"Yeah, I get that, Jerry. Just let me get under there one more time and figure out what the hell is going on." Again, he disappeared with his crew to sort out the problem.

Figuring I had to get something on film while we waited, I grabbed Chamberlain and Mifune and a handheld camera, and pulled them over to a far edge of the ruts off the main set to at least get some close-ups in before dark. With dirt flying and camera shaking, I was doing my best to get the close-ups of Blackthorne pulling Toranaga out of the crevice, all the while keeping an eye on the main set for progress.

Suddenly, through my camera lens, I saw everyone in the background of my shot running. I called, "Cut," and looked up to see no one there; everyone had raced over to what appeared to be some huge commotion on the main set.

I dropped everything and ran over to find out what the hell was going on.

Seems that when Bob was underground working on the disobedient arms and their mud- caked charges, one section had released the platforms, covering him in dirt and burying him alive! Compounding the disaster, the weight of all the well-intentioned people scrambling to get him out resulted in more dirt amassing on top this man. We were at first terror stricken, but became hopeful after we made verbal contact with Bob, who let us know he was facedown with a small pocket of air around him as he screamed for us to get him out of there!

The Japanese equivalent of 911 was called and before we knew it there were a helicopter, an ambulance, and rescue personnel hustling to free him from a potential tomb. I was beyond relieved when they finally found Bobby—conscious. He was quickly airlifted out. Reports came back from the hospital that night. While he had sustained some trauma to his back, he was not severely injured and would be okay.

I cannot think of a worse nightmare for a director than to lose a life on his set. Prayers were definitely answered that day.

Getting ready for the earthquake

It finally works!

DID SOMEONE CALL FOR A PRIEST?

That night, when the shock of our near disaster had worn off a bit, Eric, my director of photography, several others, and I met to revise the shooting schedule. We needed to postpone the slated earthquake sequence until after we'd figured out how to make it work.

We finally called the Japanese crew in to go over the altered plans for the next day.

"No, Mr. London-san, we not going to film tomorrow," stated the crew chief.

"Yes, we know today was hard, but Bobby's going to be okay," I assured him.

"No, we not going to film," he dug in.

"Look," Eric added. "We know we had the accident with the earthquake scene, but we are moving on now to shoot a different scene."

"We NOT going to work tomorrow," the crew chief defiantly insisted.

Completely baffled, we Americans passed puzzled look around the table. We couldn't just stop work!

When at last it dawned on me that something else was amiss, I asked him for an explanation. "I don't understand. *Why* aren't you working tomorrow? Is there a reason other than the accident?"

"There is *fujitsu*, Mr. London-san. We work no more," he stated emphatically, making it quite clear that this was final.

A quick check with my translator revealed that "fujitsu" means "ill omen," and that the entire crew was simply finished working on this production.

Ill omen???

It was then revealed to us that, aside from a man almost losing his life in a terrible accident, earlier that same morning a dead snake had been discovered on the set. To the Japanese, these two incidents added up to an ill omen, and they were through with the production of this film.

Again, anxious looks flew around the table, this time mixed with a tinge of panic. We couldn't just stop shooting! We had to stay on schedule!

"Okay, okay," I said in my best calm, reasoning voice. "There's an ill omen on the set. What can we do to get rid of it so we can move on?"

"You must hire a Shinto priest to perform a purification ritual to clear this set of fujitsu," he declared.

"You got it!" I practically shouted in my hurry to resolve our issue.

You could hear the sighs of relief at that table as bows were exchanged and the crew turned to leave the room.

The next morning, we went out to the location. There, we found an old bearded man in long flowing white robes chanting over a swinging basket of burning incense as he walked every inch of the set.

Once the set was thoroughly purified, much to my enormous relief we continued filming.

About six weeks later, a new scheme was hatched to get our earthquake shot. We ran heavy cords under massive dirt-piled platforms to a cable that was connected to a gigantic tractor. The platforms would release when the cable was pulled.

We rehearsed it all again and put everyone in place, and I rolled all ten cameras.

I yelled action and the tractor did the job. All the platforms opened and we successfully pulled off a hell of an earthquake without a hitch!

Robin Hood He Ain't

As the Shōgun story progresses, Mariko's husband Buntaro becomes bitterly aware of Major Blackthorne's thinly veiled affection for his wife, and challenges him to a duel of archery. Since the character Buntaro is an expert marksman, to show up his rival in this scene he adeptly picks off a small target with a hefty bow and arrow in spite of its being hidden behind a paper shoji screen. If your actor is well trained, this should be a cinch to shoot and edit.

He was not.

Simply trying to thread the bow with his badly trembling hands, with the arrow popping out of the quiver take after take after take, the writing was on the wall—this was going nowhere in a big fat hurry. Through gritted teeth, I tediously shot tiny increments of hands and fingers going through the process of loading and shooting a bow and arrow. Fine. This would've worked but for the fact that in a few months' time we had to shoot this character charging in to shoot his bow and arrow . . . on horseback.

I warned the production staff way ahead of time that they had two choices. One, they could get the actor properly and thoroughly trained to shoot or two, they could go hire the best archery expert in all of Japan to double him. Confident that I was covered either way, I got back to the work at hand.

Months passed and we got set to shoot the epic scene of expert marksman Buntaro charging in on horseback, firing away with his bow and arrow.

I arrived early on set to make sure everything was in order.

"We've got another NFW on our hands today, pal," said Eric as he handed me a cup of coffee.

"No way, Eric. I told them exactly what I wanted a long time ago, and I was very clear."

He just smiled and shook his head.

With cameras ready to roll, a shout of action brought the actor—who had been training for months—charging out mounted atop his mighty steed. Great.

Buntaro loaded . . . and fumbled . . . and arrow after arrow plummeted to the ground below him.

"Don't worry about it, it's okay. We're covered," I told him, while calling production for the expert double.

With bow and arrow in hand, out stepped a precisely costumed Buntaro in the body of a shriveled little eighty-five-year-old man! I got the best expert archer in all of Japan, all right. I also got the OLDEST expert archer in all of Japan!

Quickly defaulting to my "make this work" methodology, I scrambled over to take a look at the old man's hands. To my astonishment, they were beautiful with supple, youthful, unlined skin! I was in luck!

We reloaded the cameras again and got ready to shoot my aged ace for the dynamic showdown between suitor and scorned husband.

Upon the shout of "Action," our expert marksman raised his bow, deftly lifted an arrow from his pack, smoothly placed it in the quiver, drew it back, and fired the bow right out of the frame. Yes, you read it right. He fired the bow out of the scene with the arrow still in his hands!

I froze, dumbfounded. How could that even happen? If we had a blooper reel, this would be the opener!

I managed to shoot enough tight takes on his hands, angling the shots to avoid his face, to make it work.

To say my editing experience paid off in my directing career could be the understatement of all time.

I'D LIKE A SMALL CUP, PLEASE

We were simultaneously shooting a version of *Shōgun* for the foreign markets, which required a nude scene of Mariko in the bathtub. Actress Yoko Shimada did not want to do it.

No big deal, I thought. *We'll just get a body double and shoot from her back over her shoulder, do a little editing and then we'll have what we need for both films.*

With casting directors and production managers assuring us that finding a body double for the slender and petite Yoko Shimada would be no problem, Eric and I found ourselves on a bullet train out of Kyoto headed to Tokyo to interview and cast a "nude model."

Admittedly, this part of the workload was exempt from the all of the aforementioned hardships.

In order to clearly represent the integrity of this project, Eric and I got a suite in the best hotel in Tokyo. We did not want the hunt for a nude actress to be misinterpreted in any way.

We had appointments booked all day Saturday to see stand-ins for Mariko's body double.

The first two women to arrive with their manager were promptly invited to be seated on the couch to discuss the job. A few sentences into the interview, we realized that, except for Eric and me, not one person in the room spoke a word of English.

How exactly does one communicate, "Go undress in the bathroom and come out with a towel you can drop to the floor so we can have a look at your buck-naked ass."

Hmmm. This presented a bit of a dilemma. You can't just call the front desk and ask them how to tell the women in your room to get naked in Japanese, now, can you?

Eric and I sat silently, puzzling over our predicament.

"I know," I said. "Let's call the production office back in Kyoto and get them to translate for us."

Eric brightened. Great idea.

He quickly dialed the office. The phone on the other end of the line just rang and rang. It was Saturday, nobody was at the office. Pre-cellphone days, remember?

Now what do we do?

The long pauses and bantering between Eric and me only made the awkward silences with our guests that much more awkward. With three pairs of suspicious eyes staring at us from across the room, I began to shift in my seat.

"Well, you're the producer. Just tell them!" I finally shot at Eric.

"Meee? You're the director! Why don't *you* tell them?" Eric fired back.

With this exchange, looks of skepticism flew between the manager and his two actresses.

To hell with it.

With the day slipping away, I jumped to my feet and, with arms flailing in all directions, managed to gesticulate the most absurd pantomime of stripping naked you can imagine.

There will be no Academy Award for Best Actor in my future, that's for certain. But I did manage to convey what we needed. The manager whispered to his clients and after some bowing, the girls took turns heading into the adjoining bathroom to disrobe.

I sat back down beside Eric, relieved to be past that communication breakdown. I reached for a shot of scotch to help recover from the mortifying embarrassment of my performance, and then settled in for the business of getting the part cast.

When the girls came out and the towels dropped, what followed can only be described as a classic "spit-take."

These women revealed something only found in a plastic surgeon's office brochure. Both proudly displayed sets of enormous, highly synthetic boobs. Not remotely what we needed to double for the natural, 16th century body of Mariko.

Some fourteen actresses and at least seven rounds of my ridiculous charade later, we finally found a girl who fit the bill, possessing the natural, petite shape we were looking for.

The next day, Eric and I hopped on the train back to Kyoto. We arrived on the set Monday morning, and promptly handed the photo of our body double to the casting department. We asked them to book her for the bath scene, which we would be shooting in two short weeks.

Phew, problem number 1,219 solved.

On the morning of the shoot, I checked in on the set, and saw Eric making his way straight toward me.

"Hey, Jer, got a minute?" he said with a disconcerted look in his eye that could only mean one thing: Trouble.

"Okay Eric, now what's wrong?" I asked, preparing for the next crisis.

"Remember that little trip we took to Tokyo?" he said.

"Yep."

"Remember that hilarious pantomime you did and everything?"

"Yes, Eric, I remember," I said, beginning to grow impatient.

"And remember that petite girl we finally found in all those . . ."

"Yes, Eric, yes! I remember!" I snapped. "Now, what the heck is going on?"

"Well, why dontcha come with me?" he said with a little smirk.

I followed him down a hall and over into the makeup room. There, in a chair, getting prepped for the shoot, was our body double for Mariko. A large girl I'd never laid eyes on before with the biggest bazooms I had ever seen in my life. I mean, these things could serve as bumper pads for the Queen Mary.

"What the hell???" I blurted, darting out of the room.

"Seems the girl we picked was busy, so Japanese casting just figured you'd like this one," Eric said with a wry smile.

"I can't possibly shoot her, Eric!"

"I know, I know. Just try and shoot as much as you can, and I'll get on it and see what I can do," he said calmly. Eric, Problem Solver.

I set about shooting the bath scene with Blackthorne and Mariko over her shoulder, stalling for time as best I could. With Eric the Fixer's help, we had another more proportionally appropriate girl step into the bathtub at 5:00 p.m. to complete the shot.

Once again, our cultural disconnect had presented itself.

There exists an ironic dichotomy in Japanese culture. Socially, personal conduct is quite conservative, and conforming behavior is strictly adhered to. Their views on sexuality, on the other hand, are strikingly permissive and liberal.

In our case, it seems casting just assumed that if Americans were going to shoot a nude woman, we would want to film the modern, manufactured incarnation of the female form. They missed the point entirely.

Mariko's body double

ABOUT FACE

Nearing the end of the shoot, with the budget escalating skyward, we had to look for ways to start trimming expenses. We had eleven drivers on salary—most of them sitting around with nothing to do—so that seemed a simple and obvious place to make some necessary cutbacks.

Once again, incongruent protocol reared its burdensome head. You see, in Japan, if you hire someone for a production—no matter the position—you hire them for the entire production. Termination prior to completion of service is simply not an option. We learned this the hard way.

When our production manager resisted, emphatically declaring that he refused to pay drivers for sitting around doing nothing, we thought that would be the end of that.

We thought wrong.

The day after his declaration, the set was a very lonely place. No lighting, no camera, no makeup, no one in wardrobe—not one single member of the crew showed up. Not one! It was a total shutdown of production! We were forced to relent and pay the drivers to do absolutely nothing just to finish the production.

While busy getting spectacular film, our cultural schism only continued to rupture.

On Japanese production crews, it's the prop man who attends to various wants and needs of the director. I heard the word "no" in Japan more than any other word, mostly from the mouth of my Japanese prop man.

The response to any request was always an emphatic, "No, we can't get it." If I wanted a specific sword for authenticity in a certain scene, the answer was, "No, we can't get it." Being that it was hotter than hell in this part of Japan during the summer, even the benign request for ice in my drinks always generated the same answer. "No, we can't get it."

Apparently, it never settled well with them that the director of this epic story of Japanese civilization wasn't Japanese.

No matter how large or small the call, the daggers in my prop man's eyes exhibited a perplexing contempt for me.

"This can't go on, Eric," I lamented to my comrade-in-arms. "I can't get *any*thing. It's really slowing things down. I've had to badger the guy since July for something as simple as ice!"

Eric just shrugged. "What are you gonna do? You know the rules. You can't fire anybody here."

Resigning myself to the fact that he was right, I just stuffed it and moved on.

The next day we were working on the soundstage, shooting an insert of ninjas climbing the castle walls for the attack. We shot what we could of the exteriors on location at the castle, but the actual close-ups of the ninja's hooks had to be done on a soundstage.

The assistant directors were down on the floor throwing hooks into walls while I perched atop a great big ladder to oversee the shots of the hooks going into the wall from above.

Suddenly from below I heard screaming in Japanese. It was so loud, so piercing that I couldn't continue with the shot. I had to cut it to find out what the hell was going on.

Through a hasty translation from my interpreter, I learned that it was my friend the prop man, mad as hell at the assistant directors because *they* were throwing the ninja hooks into the wall and it was *his* job to throw the ninja hooks into the wall so he decided to unleash his fury at them then and there, right in the middle of my take!

Anyone who knows me will tell you that I am by nature soft-spoken and very slow to anger.

Except for that day.

I felt the Dragon of Japanese lore consume me. With blood boiling, flames coming out of my ears, and steam coming out of my nose . . .

I. Totally. Lost. It.

"You get that motherfucker off my stage!" I erupted. "Now! I don't EVER want to see that prick again as long as I live! I don't give a shit what the fucking rules are. Get him out!!!!"

I had simply snapped. On and on I raged from the top of my ladder, when I noticed—and tried to ignore—a tugging at my pant leg.

"What? Whaaaat?" I snarled. "I've *had it* with this shit and I am NOT gonna put up with it anymore!" The dam had broken and I was on a roll.

"Jerry, Jerry! Calm down!" It was Eric.

"I want that asshole out of here NOW!" I screamed.

"Yeah, yeah, I get it," a rattled Eric sputtered. "But I thought I should tell you that the *New York Times* is on the set today. They're right over there," he whispered, pointing to a dark corner, "and they are taking down every word you're saying."

Oops.

Two weeks later I got a copy of the *New York Times*. The headline of the Entertainment pages blared, "Unrest on the *Shōgun* Set." They told the whole story word for accurate word.

I had to do some serious tap dancing to pacify the executives back home at Paramount.

Of course, losing face is not an option to the Japanese, and word of my meltdown on the set quickly got around. The next day the Japanese production exec hauled the prop man into my office to formally "apologize" to me.

I will never forget watching this man's lips move as I sat there listening to my interpreter translate into English his exacting, methodically crafted apology. His eyes, however, shouted something very different, filling the room with nothing but disdain and contempt for me. In spite of his true feelings for me, he was bound to his cultural code of conduct. Therefore, as decorum dictated, he was required to "apologize" for his behavior. He accomplished his mission. He had "saved face."

I thanked him and let it go at that.

It seems to me that it would've been a whole lot easier for the guy if he had just brought me the damned ice for my drinks!

And as for the rest of us, when in Japan you, too, *will* comply with Japanese policy. Can you believe I never did get rid of that prop man?

A CRACK IN THE CEILING

As hot as the summer was in Japan, I think the biting cold of winter was even harder to take. Likely both perceptions were amplified by the fact that encounters with both air-conditioning and heating on cavernous sound stages were practically nonexistent.

As we were finishing up late one frigid December night on a soundstage in Kyoto, working on the very last scene of the entire film, I happened to glance down. I noticed an odd dot on the floor that was clearly not an intentional mark placed by the crew.

Looking up, I realized there was a crack in the ceiling above that allowed a tiny sliver of moonlight to stream in.

As the scene came to an end, I vividly remember hearing the word "cut" leave my lips for the last time. The entire shoot, all six and one half months of it, had been at once enthralling and tortuous—a dizzying ride of disasters and victories.

It had been a hard-fought personal battle to maintain my own equilibrium, but with so many people counting on me to deliver the goods, I'd had to dig deep to end up standing there at that moment.

Not that it was ever a goal for me, but I am proud to say that our scheduled one-hundred-and-forty-day undertaking was completed in one hundred and thirty-five days. This accomplishment was made possible in no small part by the expertise of Director of Photography Andy Laszlo, Art Director Joe Jennings, and Japanese Art Director Shin Nishida, who won an Emmy for *Shōgun*. Together we managed to get some of the greatest production values ever seen on television, even rivaling those seen in feature films.

The journey had also exploited the limits of my family's ability to endure, and mine to maintain the fortitude to accomplish an enormous project. I could scarcely reconcile the fact that with that last shout of "cut," it was over, it was finished, it was complete.

Drawn toward that little dot on the floor, I will never forget stepping into that bright stream of moonlight, which had ended its long journey from the moon to the floor just as I had ended my own long journey right there in that same spot.

I made it. I actually made it.

And I lived through it, with tales to tell.

OFF WITH THEIR HEADS!

O ne advantage of the limited technology in those days is that, as dailies didn't arrive in the States until at least a week after they were shot in Japan, the studio rarely interfered in anything we did. It was always too late.

Although we had edited while filming, we spent an additional eight months at Paramount with five editors working fulltime to put the massive film together.

But it was the huge stink that arose after the final cut went to NBC that had us wondering if they'd ever even read the script!

There were two scenes, very dynamic, intense but integral to the story, that Eric included in the script. We worked hard to shoot both as sensitively and as tastefully as we could without diminishing the impact those scenes made in the unfolding of James Clavell's story.

One scene was that of a Japanese soldier suffering the consequences of an improper bow to his commander, and paying the price for his digression with his beheading.

The other scene also dealt with the cost of disrespect to a superior, this time by Major Blackthorne, whose punishment was being urinated upon by his commander.

I'd had a good deal of experience shooting for American television by this time, and was no stranger to the sensibilities of Standard and Practices regarding censorship. But let me tell you, when the network saw these two scenes, they flipped! Eric and I, as well as Mr. Clavell himself, all stood firm on this one. There was going to be no bastardizing of this story whatsoever. I'm quite sure that ultimately the wonderful NBC executive Ethel Winant stepped in to help convince the network of our resolve and to influence the ultimate outcome, which was to leave in the controversial scenes just as we had shot them. I had worked with Ethel before, and always knew she had my back.

As you might well imagine, what we shot in those two scenes doesn't hold a candle to what we regularly see on primetime television today. Since then, I've seen soap commercials on TV that are far more provocative than both of those scenes put together!

Behead mockup

The beheading

Before we returned home, my wife and I went to Bangkok where, for one of the first times in my life, I became very ill. I think my body just collapsed once the weight of my responsibilities was removed. Nevertheless, we stayed for a week, while I gorged myself on steak, lobster, and any kind of Western food I hadn't had in almost a year, trying to recuperate and prepare for re-entry into a life back in the States that I scarcely remembered.

Nothing I can say here could overstate the impact *Shōgun* had on me, the cast, our crew, and even our country as a whole.

When *Shōgun* aired in September of 1980, it took an unprecedented 60% of market shares in the Nielsen ratings for five straight nights. Theaters all across the country sat dark that week, suffering heavy losses. Sushi restaurants, which were basically unheard of in the West, sprouted overnight like mushrooms. Likewise, martial arts studios. There was even a surge of American men traveling to Japan with the sole intent of bringing home a Japanese bride!

As *Shōgun* racked up Emmy Awards for Outstanding Limited Series, Art Direction, and Main Title Design, the Golden Globe Award, my award from the Directors Guild of America for Outstanding Director, and the Peabody Award for Cultural Advancement that year, I was now being offered an immense number of projects. Hiring Salli Newman to help me produce, I struck a deal with CBS: For every two projects I did for them, I could direct and produce my own project. They agreed to greenlight any project I truly believed in.

For all it brought to—and took from—my life, *Shōgun* remains the work am I most proud of.

Shōgun Emmy

Shōgun DGA Award

Emmy Magazine

SNOW AND ICE IN MIAMI

The international attention my career garnered as a result of *Shōgun* was astonishing. Some of it was welcome. Some of it . . . not so much.

Shortly after *Shōgun* was released, I was invited to Florida by an American filmmaker who wanted me to direct a story about the burgeoning drug smuggling operations in South America. Given that the United States' emerging challenges with the drug trade had just started to come to light, a well-timed tale of international subterfuge could be fascinating. Intrigued by the idea, I accepted the invitation and headed to Miami.

I met the filmmaker and his lovely blond wife for dinner at the beautiful restaurant overlooking the harbor of a private yacht club. Halfway through our appetizers, we were joined by a heavily pregnant woman and her brother, a menacing fellow with piercing dark eyes and a hefty gold nugget watch strapped to his wrist. Our host then began to reveal more details of the story for the film.

It seems that in the midst of increasing bloodshed in Columbia, there was a particular drug lord who, in semi-Robin Hood-esque style, bestowed a few fragments of his massive wealth upon smaller towns and villages that had been ravaged by drug trade violence. Apparently, he was seen by many of the impoverished as a hero.

As this benevolent criminal's story unfolded, the pregnant woman just smiled. Her brother glared.

My very enthusiastic host went on to tell me that he and the man who would be the subject of the film had been extremely impressed by *Shōgun*, and had decided I was the one they wanted to direct the cinematic telling of this tale. He apologized that the film's hero was "unavailable" and could not join us that evening.

While he continued to recite the accomplishments and exploits of his main character over dinner, emphasizing that no expense would be spared in the making of this film, I found myself slightly distracted by the enormous diamonds displayed on each and every one of the expectant mother's fingers. As in Harry-Winston-has-nothing-left-in-the-store-to-sell type of diamonds.

The woman was silent most of the night except for when she expressed in broken English her regrets that her husband wasn't with us. She explained that she was there without him because she wanted to have her baby in America rather than in Columbia due to the superior healthcare services the U.S. provided.

I pointed out to my host that I was only the director, and that a qualified writer would have to be hired to pen the story before it could be made into a film.

Not a problem, he said without blinking an eye.

"Hola, Carlos!" The filmmaker rose to greet the young man approaching our table. "You are just in time to take our guest on a little tour of your boat."

Welcoming the opportunity to grab some fresh air and clear my head a bit, I followed the young man—probably all of twenty years old—out to the docks below the restaurant's massive windows. We stopped beside an imposing, one hundred fifty-foot, highly polished, gleaming, three-masted, multi-million-dollar teak schooner.

Rarely have I encountered such exorbitance, and when I have, it has usually been accompanied by blood the color of blue. Since there are limited ways to acquire the ostentatious wealth on display that night, I stood on the dock beginning to devise a plan to get the hell out of Dodge!

As I boarded the boat, Carlos reached over and threw open concealed hatches to proudly show off the vessel's state-of-the-art electronics. "Es easy," he boasted with a snigger. "I signal to my friends at de Coast Guard dat we are coming into American waters, den my little boats meet me at sea to unload de cargo, den dey scatter and I go on my way. The DEA don' know nothing."

Okaaaay, then. Time to get back to dinner. Preferably at home three thousand miles away.

I headed back to restaurant. Following dessert, my host invited me to the menacing brother's palatial estate nearby for an after-dinner drink. Thinking a good stiff nightcap was exactly what I could use at that moment, I accepted.

After the twenty-year-old scotch was poured into the finest cut crystal glasses, my host and the brutish brother beckoned me over to a very large billiard table. Fears that I'd be challenged to a pool stick duel with Mr. Sunshine vanished when the table's enormous cover was flung aside. There, blanketing the entire table, were two-foot-high stacks of one hundred dollar bills. I guessed there had to be about ten million dollars there.

Oh, gee. Will you look at the time!

Politely excusing myself—oh, you know, jet lag and all—I reassured my host that I'd love to direct his film, then raced back to my room. *Okay, figure your way out of* this one, *Mr. Director*, I thought as I paced the room trying to stifle my panic. *White powder and toe tags are definitely NOT your style.*

Hardly able to sleep anyway, I bolted out of bed at around three a.m. to the sound of approaching sirens. Peering from my window, I could see through the dim light that the man on the stretcher headed for the ambulance was followed by my host's lovely blond wife. I popped my head out the window as they passed; she assured me that her husband's anxiety attacks were nothing unusual, and that he would be just fine.

And there was my cue . . . exit stage left! I grabbed the phone and called the airline. Dallas, Des Moines, Podunk, I don't care. Just get me on the next flight out of Miami!

I left a respectful note to my host, expressing my gratitude for his generosity and wishes for his speedy recovery. Hoping that requests for a writer for this nightmare would never materialize, I set off for the airport.

I was soon reminded that hope is not a strategy.

A month later, the phone rang. It was my host, inquiring about the list of writers I had promised him. I assured him I would get it to him as soon as possible.

And that's exactly what I did.

He received from my agent a list of the most illustrious, most awarded, most expensive, most unattainable writers in the history of the film industry.

I never heard from him again.

I was beyond relieved when that was over, but I will tell you that three-masted boats and pool tables *still* make me shudder!

I was also invited to China to explore the possibility of shooting a miniseries in Beijing. Conditions there made the *Shōgun* shoot look like a trip to the Four Seasons spa! I found stages with no floors, let alone heat. Don't even get me started on the housing facilities. Needless to say, I passed.

THE ORDEAL OF RAY SHARKEY

Ordeal of Bill Carney

The first movie I took on as producer in my new deal with CBS was called *The Ordeal of Bill Carney*. Producing, I learned, was a knife that cut both ways. It meant that I had much more freedom in the decision-making aspects, which was fantastic. On the other hand, it also meant that it was my ass on the line if things didn't go well.

So, what does a perfectly sane man do in the confines of this situation?

He hires a lead actor with a widely whispered reputation for issues with substance abuse, of course. This time in the form of Ray Sharkey.

What could possibly go wrong?

The Ordeal of Bill Carney was a compelling true story about a war hero whose tragic jeep accident left him a quadriplegic, and fighting to regain custody of his children. The cast also included brilliant actor Richard Crenna as costar.

My decision to ignore the rumors—along with some random guy's daily lunchtime visits to Ray's trailer—began to catch up with me during a scene where Ray had a long monologue in his wheelchair. With cameras rolling, he was grinding his way through the scene, talking and talking, when he simply fell asleep! Right in the middle of the scene!

Not having dealt with anything like this before, I decided to keep the cameras rolling while thinking to myself, *The boys back at CBS are just gonna love this.*

Some days Ray was . . . relaxed. Other days he was manic.

With Ray struggling to remember his lines in the over-the-shoulder two shots, Richard Crenna, seasoned professional that he was, told Ray to leave space where his lines were supposed to be. Then Richard just carried on in the scenes with dead silence from his scene partner.

By this time, the network had had enough and wanted to replace Ray. That's where the knife began to cut both ways. As a director, great news! There was headache I didn't need—gone.

On the other hand, as a producer it meant starting all over, which translated to a complete and total destruction of my budget. I decided to tough it out, a decision I would soon be kicking myself for.

With KFWB keeping me company as I slogged my way down the 405 Freeway on the predawn drive into work, a "breaking news" report came on the radio that jolted me awake more sharply than the double espresso in my mug.

Ray Sharkey had been arrested the night before for threatening his wife, and was in the county jail awaiting arraignment on battery charges.

With eight pages of his dialogue to shoot that day, I considered my options—including changing the title of this project to "The Ordeal of Jerry London."

After waiting for the "holy crap" shock of the crew to wear off, I conferred with them on the best way to shoot around Sharkey that day. Calls to his agent on his "availability" were met with the usual attempts at placation.

Right around noon, Ray rolled in. We sat him down and took turns trying to drill home to the guy that his career was hanging in the balance and that if he kept it up, he'd be finished, not only on this shoot but in the entire industry! Of course, all the fatherly wisdom coming his way was met with the requisite and predictable contrition and apologies.

As history will tell, nothing really changed for him, but somehow I managed to get through the shoot and complete the movie.

While a good case could be made against the sanity and logic of my decisions, it couldn't hold a candle to the irony of my intuition.

Ray Sharkey was nominated for a Golden Globe Award for his performance.

Three years later, I was working on a project in Rome when who walked right into the elevator at my hotel?

Yep. Ray Sharkey.

"Jerry Jerry, wow, great to see you!" he beamed. "I'm shooting a picture with Anthony Quinn. What are you doing here?"

"I'm working on a film with Gregory Peck. Great to see you working and looking well, Ray," I responded, glad to see him straight.

"Oh, hey, Jer. I know I was a real bad boy on our last picture. I really want to apologize to you for that," he said sheepishly.

"Well, it's good to see you sober, Ray," I replied. "Congrats and good luck on your film." I waved as he exited the elevator.

He was a terrific actor.

Three or four days later, I was heading back to my room after just finishing a night shoot. Again, Ray popped into the elevator.

"Hey Ray, how's it going?" I smiled.

His response was so incoherent I could scarcely understand it. I felt a hard knot form in my stomach as I watched him struggle just to stand.

Sadly, we all know this story had no happy ending. After numerous attempts at rehabilitation, Sharkey died of complications from the AIDS virus he reportedly contracted through drug use.

LONDON AND THE VATICAN

I got my hands on a script CBS had that was written by David Butler, called *The Scarlet and The Black*. I fell in love with it. It was a true story set in Rome during World War II about a Vatican priest hiding downed pilots, escaped POWs, and Italian resistance families. His actions resulted in a Nazi plan to assassinate him. The story was brilliant and engaging, and with a cast like Gregory Peck, Christopher Plummer, and Sir John Gielgud attached, it was a dream come true. I just *had* to do it.

The Scarlet and the Black

133

GREGORY PECK stars as the man who led thousands in a daring escape to freedom— right under the nose of the Gestapo.

THE SCARLET and THE BLACK

Based on a true story • WORLD TELEVISION PREMIERE! also starring CHRISTOPHER PLUMMER and SIR JOHN GIELGUD

Written by David Butler • Directed by Jerry London

8PM CBS⊗2

A CBS SPECIAL 3-HOUR MOTION PICTURE EVENT

I lobbied the executives at CBS hard for it. In the end, the word was that *if* Mr. Peck—who had never heard of me—approved me, then and only then was I in.

The tables had turned. The director had to audition for the actor!!

The meeting with Gregory Peck, essentially my audition, was to take place at his beautiful home in Holmby Hills. And, yes, I was nervous!

I was met at the door by his butler, whom I followed into a large living room, where I was left to wait for Mr. Peck. Too antsy to sit, I stood gazing out of a huge picture window, mesmerized by a gorgeous view of expansive rolling lawns that seemed to go on forever.

I didn't notice as Mr. Peck entered the room.

"Jerry, I'm happy to meet you" boomed that deep, smoky, unmistakable voice.

Startled, I turned to see that familiar, tall, broad-shouldered man silhouetted by the foyer as Gregory Peck made his way toward me. He greeted me warmly, and we sat down and chatted for quite some time about the fantastic script of *The Scarlet and The Black*. Then it was over.

I left what felt to me like a good meeting, with fingers tightly crossed.

Soon the call came that Mr. Peck had done his homework and research on me. As a result, shortly after our meeting, approval was granted.

All I can say is: Thank God I passed the audition. Again, this gave me a deeper understanding of how actors feel!

When I first met Sir John Gielgud, the extraordinary British actor who was to play Pope Pius, I was instantly struck by his warmth and approachability, a stark contrast to what I guess I had been expecting from this Oscar, Emmy, Tony, and Grammy-winning knighted master of Shakespeare.

Sir John Gielgud and Jerry

Following my own form of gushing over his work, including expressions of my gratitude to be working with such a legend, his response was so humble and gracious that it put me instantly at ease.

135

"Jerry, I don't want you to be afraid to talk to me," he said, with words rolling melodically off his tongue. "If I am speaking too slowly, kindly tell me. If I need to pick up the pace, tell me that, as well."

This wasn't exactly what I'd been expecting to hear from one of the greatest actors that ever graced the stage, but as my experience has repeatedly shown me, the bigger they are, the more gracious, generous, and professional they are to work with.

There was a part in *The Scarlet and the Black* that I thought would be wonderful for the legendary Italian actress, Gina Lollobrigida.

The first meeting with this screen legend went a little differently. She invited the producer and me to her home. Ever the gracious hostess, she led us on a tour of her beautiful abode, which included her eye-popping ruby-red velvet-wallpapered and mirror-ceilinged bedroom.

She passed on the film, but I will always be able to truthfully claim that I was once in Gina Lollobrigida's bedroom!

I had a fantastic crew for this film, including my daughter Lisa, who was employed as a production assistant. I also had Director of Photography Giuseppe Rittono and Assistant Director and lifelong friend Gianni Cozzo, the best there ever was. That lifelong friendship was not nearly long enough. Gianni died of a heart attack at only forty-nine years of age.

After months of negotiations between our producers and the Vatican, we were granted permission to shoot inside the Vatican for three days—an illustrious asset to the film, indeed!

The night before we began the Vatican shoot, word citing security concerns reached me that our three-day permission had been withdrawn. We would only be allowed to shoot for one day on the premises.

That left me with two highly undesirable choices and only hours to make the necessary adjustments to either one: Cut the script, or somehow impossibly cram three days' worth of shooting into one day.

Of course, I chose the latter.

I stayed up all night rearranging sixty different setups. Enlisting three camera crews and three assistant directors, I arranged a dovetail from one shot to the next. With the most graciously accommodating professionalism of Gregory Peck, who was in and out of more than twenty of those scenes, we managed to get every shot we needed, sacrificing none of the incomparable Vatican splendor while simultaneously maintaining the integrity of the script.

You could say it was our own miracle at the Vatican!

The Vatican

Jerry and Greg, the nun

Monsignor Peck and Jerry

In the opening scene of the film, a German staff car rolls into St. Peter's Square carrying a Nazi General and his assistant. They get out of the car and ascend the steps of the Vatican to meet with the Pope.

As one of the most frequented tourist destinations in the world, St. Peter's Square is an extremely busy place, with tour busses loaded with "the faithful" from all over the world arriving every day at 7:30 a.m. on the dot. Even with a 5:00 a.m. call time, this left me with a very tight window to get the shot done between dawn and 7:30. To my relief, things were going along very smoothly until . . .

"Jerry, we've got a problem," frowned Gianni Cozzo, my first assistant director and right-hand man. "The general's assistant's boots are missing."

"No big deal," I said. "Just get another pair off one of the extras and put them on him."

"This guy's got a size thirteen shoe and there is nothing anywhere that'll fit him," he wailed.

Now I had a problem. The clock was ticking. I had about twenty minutes until the hordes of tourists invaded the space, and I HAD to get that shot. As if cramming three days of shooting into one wasn't stressful enough, I had a serious wardrobe malfunction in a defining moment of the film!

Once again, the old director's dilemma—figure it out, and fast! I could no longer do a tight shot because we'd already seen them get out of the car and climb the front steps.

Taking a deep breath while trying to clear my head, I scanned the set and saw everyone waiting for me to tell them what to do next. I looked around at the multitude of extras in period streetwear, at Christopher Plummer and Walter Gotell in their resplendent black uniforms with medals gleaming in the early morning light, stiff caps on their heads, knee high black boots and . . . their knee-high black socks! Then it hit me! Nobody would ever know the difference!

"Back up the cameras. Quick! And let's shoot!" I called to my first-rate director of photography, Giuseppe Rotunno. After a few puzzled looks and a swift repositioning of the cameras, up the grand stairs to the Vatican stomped the perfectly polished general and his assistant in his black knee-high socks. With the click of boots hitting pavement in postproduction sound effects, no one was ever the wiser!

PECK, PLUMMER, AND PINCH ME

Jerry at the Colosseum

This shoot held one of the most amazing "pinch me" moments I had ever experienced in my career. We had been cleared to shoot inside the Roman Colosseum at night. I had two cameras and ten to twelve different angles to get.

The scene was a piercing, intense ten pages between Gregory Peck and Christopher Plummer—one pleading with the other for the salvation of his family. The potency of the dialogue in the hands of these two giants of the screen was beyond powerful.

The atmosphere was simply mind blowing.

As the scene unfolded, I had one of those "How the hell did I get here?" reality checks. I was standing in the eternal stillness of the ancient Roman Colosseum in the dead of night beneath a full moon, watching close up two of the greatest actors who had ever lived just killing it. I remember gazing up to the heavens in unspoken gratitude for a once-in-a-lifetime moment no one had a right to expect.

The performances of those men that night were nothing less than perfection, and I printed take one on every single shot.   A true "Is this really happening to me?" moment, for sure.

Compounding the sheer joy of working on this project was the score of the brilliant composer and Academy Award winner, Ennio Morricone, who incidentally never spoke a word of English. We communicated entirely through his translator, and he produced a fabulous score for the film, adding the icing on the cake to a truly magical experience.

Plummer, Peck, and Gielgud

A HOTEL FOR AARON SPELLING

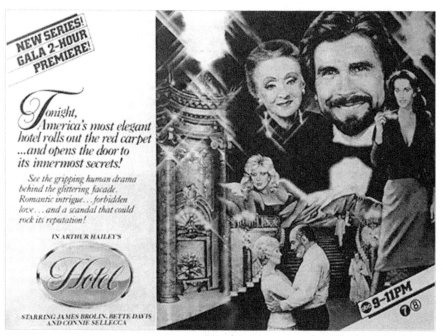

Hotel

A t this point in time, my life was pretty sweet; the family was healthy, the kids were in college, my career was gliding along nicely.

So Marilynn and I decided to buy a little getaway place in the desert. We settled on a condo inside the Rancho Las Palmas development in Rancho Mirage near Palm Springs. She was happy because she was next to great shopping. I was happy because I was next to great golf.

Friends are easily made when you come to the desert seeking relaxation, and I found myself playing a good bit of tennis with Bob Small, the general manager of the Rancho Las Palmas Marriott Resort hotel right next to our condo. Bobby and his wife were frequent dinner guests of ours, as I was lucky enough to marry a woman who not only held a black belt in shopping but also a black belt in cooking. Bobby loved to talk about movies and whatever news and gossip were front and center in entertainment that week.

"Jer, you really ought'a do a show about hotels," Bobby piped up one evening over cocktails before dinner. "I'm telling you, it'd be a hit."

"What's so exciting about hotels?" I said. "People check in, people check out. Boring."

With a second gin and tonic in hand, the stories that came flowing out of Bobby about the inner life of hotels were nothing less than stunning. There were unique discoveries: a dead body, a suitcase full of cash, an errant python. There were dramatic encounters: a wife and the "other woman" meeting in the lobby, skimming employees, secret prostitutes, tangled staff love affairs, etcetera, etcetera. All this got me thinking that maybe the inner life of a hotel wouldn't be so boring after all.

"I know the perfect hotel to shoot, too, Jer," Bobby said with the enthusiasm of a kid with a new toy. "The Fairmont in San Francisco. What a grand old beauty!"

Deciding there could be something to this television hotel idea after all, but also fully aware that a movie called *Hotel* based on the book by Arthur Hailey already existed, I asked my assistant Mike Callaway to go get a copy of the movie.

Mike, being a struggling writer, was happy to comply with my request to take the characters out of the movie and do an outline for a TV series. Who knows, maybe we could sell it. He worked hard on the outline. Since we had taken our concept from the book, we made it a point during presentation to say, "This is Arthur Hailey's *Hotel* as a series." We did not make it our own.

Glen Larson would be so disappointed in me.

I took the outline to my agent at the high-powered Creative Artists Agency. He really liked the treatment and offered me his take on it right away. "Well, we can go shop it around, or we can give it to Aaron Spelling (the king of such wildly successful shows such as *90210* and *Charlie's Angels*), and it will run for years. Your choice," he flatly stated. ""But I have to tell you, Jerry, if you're on for five years, your end of the profits as creator will be well over a million dollars."

"Well, what kind of choice is that?" I said, delighted. "Let's give it to Aaron!"

I met with Mr. Spelling. He was very personable and he really liked the treatment.

After the meeting, I got Bobby on the phone. "Hey Bobby, you got your wish. We're gonna do a pilot about a hotel. Keep those stories coming!"

"Aww, that's just great, Jer!"

"By the way, how do I get into the Fairmont in San Francisco?"

"I know the manager up there," Bobby gushed, quite proud to be a part of that link to the Hollywood that so fascinated him. "I'll give him a call for you."

The Vice President of The Fairmont was accommodating . . . to a point. We were in, but with one condition: During the week allotted to us for our location shoot, we were restricted to shooting only between the hours of 11:00 p.m. and 5:00 a.m.

Having faced far greater challenges than that, I didn't see a problem.

My art director, my set decorator, and I took stock. The guest rooms, and of course the lobby, were just beautiful.

We worked out a tight schedule to shoot all the interiors; we had to get the lobby stuff, entrances, exits, etc. Of course, the exteriors could wait because we could get shots of the hotel and beauty shots of San Francisco whenever we wanted to. We would shoot inside the hotel Thursday and do the final exteriors on Friday, our last day.

Or so we thought.

With all the interiors done and one day left to shoot and finish off the exteriors, it started to rain. Hard.

Fine, Mr. Director. We've been here before. Plan. Foil. Pivot. Succeed.

"Tell Aaron we need another day," I told his assistant in L.A. as I watched the relentlessly dark skies pour buckets all over my Friday schedule.

"Sorry Jerry. You can't stay. You've got to head back," he said.

"You gotta give me another day! I'll do it in half a day!" I pleaded. "Just give me five hours and I'll get the essential shots!"

Only the sound of the pounding rain outside my window filled a long pause while I waited for what seemed like hours for a response.

"Okay, but if you don't get it then, that's IT!" came the frustrated voice on the other end of the phone.

I'm not sure I slept much that night, but San Francisco saved me when I awoke to a bright and sunny Saturday morning. I did two days of work in one day, and finished the pilot for a show that went on for six years!

Despite an enormous and brilliant cast, the non-cooperative weather and a tight, mostly-night schedule made shooting the pilot a grind. There were times that fatigue would jet past exhaustion straight into loopy.

"Hey Jerry, what say we go upstairs and grab a bedroom?" teased an equally exhausted guest star, Morgan Fairchild, at about 3:00 a.m. one night while we sat on the set waiting for lighting.

With my tongue planted firmly in cheek, I replied that I was too tired to raise a glass, let alone anything else. It was all in good fun, but a lively fantasy nevertheless, courtesy of the beautiful Ms. Fairchild.

Morgan Fairchild and Jerry—*Hotel*

Led by James Brolin and Connie Sellecca, the cast on the pilot was just amazing.

I had the privilege of directing screen legend Bette Davis, whose character, the wealthy hotel owner, was a series regular. At that point in time, I believe Miss Davis was in her late eighties. I had never before seen a work ethic quite like hers. Every single day she was on set in a little chair not far from my camera, rather than off in her dressing room relaxing like everyone else. Just a slip of a woman, she sat there every day, seemingly fascinated by watching her fellow actors work. Astoundingly, she knew everybody's lines, including her own! I watched her day after day mouthing each line of each character in each scene. Every. Single. Word. She was extraordinary.

Regrettably, ill health forced her to withdraw from the series, only to be replaced—with great irony—by Anne Baxter, her nemesis in *All About Eve*. To further that irony, Miss Baxter predeceased Miss Davis by four years!

The legendary crooner Mel Tormé just happened to be performing at the Fairmont Hotel while we were filming, so I gave him a part in the show, too.

ABC snapped *Hotel* right up and it went on for six seasons. I think the list of those who did *not* guest star on that series is much shorter than those who did. Everybody who was anybody, had been anybody, or would someday become somebody did that show! The stories we told, not unlike Bobby's, were considered quite controversial.

I made the choice to direct only the pilot, because as a creator of the show I had a royalty and deal granting me 5% of the profits.

Niiiicce!

That freed me up to pursue what was now my passion for miniseries and great TV movies. A perfect scenario, indeed.

This is when I learned about that oh-so-creative world of Hollywood accounting.

JERRY LONDON

HOW MUCH IS 2 + 2?
HOW MUCH DO YOU WANT IT TO BE?

A t the end of six blockbuster seasons, I received a statement from the accounting department at Aaron Spelling Productions stating that *Hotel* was $300,000 in the hole, but was now on its way to syndication. Fantastic.

Every year thereafter I would get a biannual statement from Aaron Spelling Productions claiming that the show had received ten million dollars in profits, but that expenses that year had been eleven million! "Production expenses" were another five million! Oh, you know how pesky those production expenses can be when the show isn't even *in* production!!

This went on for *six years* of syndication. To *this day*, that show is still "in the red," with no recorded profit.

I. Never. Saw. A. Single. Dime.

Attorneys I consulted with assured me that since CAA represented both Aaron and me, it would be me who would get the short end of the stick if I tried to pursue a legal action. I was practically guaranteed that I would enter into the costly infinite do-loop of the legal process, draining more money from my pocket than I'd ever see in the legitimate compensation I was owed. After all, Aaron Spelling was CAA's darling little cash cow.

In other words, I didn't stand a chance.

Bitterly disillusioned, it was becoming clear to me that CAA had pretty much pigeonholed my career. Ever on the hunt for good scripts, every single time I'd make a pitch for a movie, CAA would push another Spelling pilot on me, some of them not very good, either.

"You have to do it for Aaron," would be the constant refrain from "my" agents. I went along with this for a while simply because I loved working.

That work I was doing for Jerry, not for Aaron.

One pilot of Spelling's I was offered was called *MacGruder and Loud*. It was truly repetitive commercial dregs from the cop show era.

Aaron Spelling, Jerry, and Lois Chiles

I said no.

Shortly afterward, my phone was ringing with CAA agents asking when I was going to get started. I would repeat that I wasn't doing it. I ignored rumblings about "sweetening the deal," and continued looking for projects that interested me. But the calls persisted. After all, since no one had ever said "no" to Aaron Spelling, my agents were not about to start now.

Heading out my front door to play golf one day, I found a shiny new midnight-blue Porsche sitting in my driveway. A gift from Aaron.

It didn't come anywhere near close to compensation for royalties owed. Shamefully, it was the beginning *and* the end of my compensation.

Y'ALL COME BACK NOW, Y'HEAR?

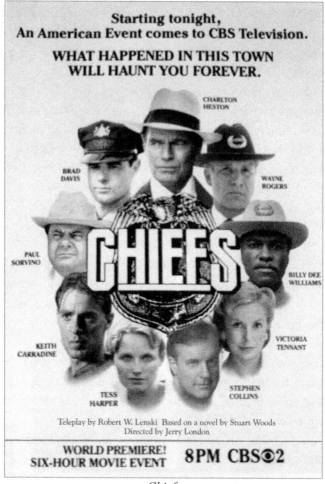

Starting tonight,
An American Event comes to CBS Television.

WHAT HAPPENED IN THIS TOWN
WILL HAUNT YOU FOREVER.

CHARLTON HESTON

BRAD DAVIS

WAYNE ROGERS

PAUL SORVINO

CHIEFS

BILLY DEE WILLIAMS

KEITH CARRADINE

VICTORIA TENNANT

TESS HARPER

STEPHEN COLLINS

Teleplay by Robert W. Lenski Based on a novel by Stuart Woods
Directed by Jerry London

WORLD PREMIERE!
SIX-HOUR MOVIE EVENT 8PM CBS◉2

Chiefs

S tuart Woods' novel, *Chiefs,* is the fascinating true story of three
generations of police officers at work in a small southern town with a
serial killer at large.

In our screen adaption of the book, we covered three periods, the
1920s, 1940s, and 1960s, all in the same town. Coming in at six hours, it

starred Charlton Heston, Billy Dee Williams, Wayne Rogers, Stephen Collins, and Victoria Tennant, alongside then-unknowns John Goodman and Danny Glover. A stellar cast with each actor totally committed to their characters. Mostly owing to massive time period changes in the same location, we shot each of the three parts separately.

When I read the script, I knew the role of the corrupt policeman Sonny Butts was perfect for Brad Davis, the phenomenal actor from one of my all-time favorite films, *Midnight Express*. He had done wonderful work in the Academy Awards Best Picture winner, *Chariots of Fire*, as well as in Robert Altman's *The Player*.

It's a tough call for a director when a role is perfect for an actor, but the actor may not be perfect for the role. To put it another way, Brad Davis had a long-standing reputation as a substance abuser, which ultimately ended up costing him dearly. Here is where a director's own form of denial can come into play. *I know this guy's a brilliant actor and just PERFECT for this part. I really, really want him, but . . .*

Well, maybe he'll behave this *time.*

Denial ain't just a river in Egypt.

Such was the case with Brad Davis.

I had cast the entire film by this point, and had considered other actors in the Sonny Butts role, but I just couldn't get Brad out of my mind. So one day I arranged to meet him for lunch where, not surprisingly, I received the predictable round of a junkie's well-rehearsed promises and placations.

Memories of my elevator rides with Ray Sharkey in Rome kept haunting me after that lunch, so I forced myself to look at other options. Robert Blake came to mind, so I met with him long enough to be reminded that, while nice enough, the guy had major control issues.

I couldn't shake Brad Davis from my mind. Few performances had ever affected me the way his did in *Midnight Express*.

I set up another lunch with him.

"Jerry, I can do this," Brad pleaded. "I tell you, I'm clean."

"Look," I said, staring hard into his eyes. "I'd really like to give you a chance because I know you'll kill the part. It's practically written for you, but I'm not just the director, I'm also the producer on this show. If you mess this up, we *both* go down with the ship."

"I promise I won't let you down," he said, oozing sincerity.

Brad shifted nervously in his seat as I caught the waiter's attention to get the check.

"You must understand that it's a huge risk for the network, as well," I said as I reached for my credit card. "I'm not even sure I can convince them to take you. And since I wear both director and producer hats on this thing, I would have to beat the crap out of *myself* if I got this wrong. If, and I mean *if*, I can get their buy in, the part is yours. Don't make me regret it."

Tears sprang to his eyes upon hearing those words, and I left that lunch glad I was giving the guy a second chance. But the dark memory of an elevator ride in Rome persisted.

I was successful in convincing the network, and Brad was cast. My gut instinct just wouldn't let go of those intense eyes and that powerful stature that told me Brad Davis was the only one to play Sonny Butts.

We set up camp in a little town called Chester in South Carolina. Population about 6,000, and I think we must have employed the entire town on that shoot. Caterers, painters, extras, drivers, gardeners—you name it. Anybody and everybody who wanted to work on the film was given the opportunity to do so.

I can tell you it's true what they say about Southern hospitality. Hardly a day went by that one of the neighbors on the little street of our rental house did not drop by with a pie or extend an invitation to dinner. I even got to sample some authentic Southern backyard moonshine. Chester embraced us all as family, even going as far as to name a park in the center of their town "Chiefs Park." Marilynn was happy to get cooking lessons in genuine down-home Southern cuisine from ladies with generations rooted in the South. On the occasional weekend, I found myself on the tennis courts opposite the truly affable Charlton Heston. I was going to hate for this shoot to end!

As we were nearing the close of the first two-hour segment, the producer John Quill paid me a visit on the set. Evidently, my reputation for winning my races with the clock had preceded me.

"Hey Jerry, looks like you're really moving along here. Do you think you can bring this one in a day under?" he asked with a hopeful twinkle in his eye.

"Yeah, I'm pretty sure I can," I said, as I just happened to be running ahead of schedule anyway.

"If you do," he said, stepping in a little closer, "we'll take care of you with a little gift."

"Well, if it's little, make it a Rolex!" I laughed. "Nah, seriously, I don't care about a gift. If I can do it, I will. If I can't, I can't." I said, dismissing the gesture.

Of course, I finished a day early, and thought nothing of it; it's just the way I work.

Shortly after we started shooting the second episode, John appeared again, and sat down next to me during a lunch break on the set. "Here you go," he said, stuffing a crumpled white napkin into my hand.

"What's this? Dessert?" I laughed.

"Go ahead. Open it," he said.

I unwrapped the wrinkled mass to find a gold Rolex. Somewhat surprised that the Rolex gag was still going, I thanked him for the obviously counterfeit watch and went back to work.

Later that day, I handed the watch to my assistant to take to a jeweler downtown to see if I could even expect the damned thing to keep time. Everyone can use a spare watch. The report came back that the watch in the wadded-up napkin did indeed keep time, because it was an authentic Rolex! Shocked the heck out of me!

Brad Davis really had me sweating it on his first few days on set. Was I about to pay a hefty price for a wish I had granted? For a vision I hadn't been able to let go of?

I could quickly see that he was turning in first-rate work. His commanding interpretation of Sonny Butts was just what I had envisioned, so I relaxed. A little.

We were winding down near the end of the shoot. On this particular day, Brad was finishing his last scene, a highly emotional one between him and his mother, who was played by Kaiulani Lee.

When the scene was over and the customary announcement was made for an actor's last day on set of, "That's a wrap for Brad. Everyone say goodbye," the entire crew stopped what they were doing, dropped whatever was in their hands, and applauded, whistled, and cheered.

And they didn't stop.

The spontaneous ovation went on for some time. Brad, overcome, broke down into tears. He wasn't alone.

Chiefs—Brad Davis and Jerry

I had trusted my instincts and they'd paid off. Brad had kept his word and kept clean. And while this highly acclaimed project garnered numerous Emmy nominations, what took place that day on the set was far and away the most rewarding moment I'd ever had, not only as a director, but as a human being.

GIVE MY COMPLIMENTS TO THE CHEF

Somewhere in the middle of the third episode, Producer John Quill dropped by the set for another visit. "You know, Jer, if you can bring this one in a little early . . ." began his familiar refrain.

"Yeah, I know, John. I really do appreciate it, but I don't need any more goodies. I'll just get it done early if I can."

In closing out part three, with good planning and a fast crew, things again proceeded very well, and again I finished a day early.

We did all the editing on the film in New York; Marilynn was more than happy to accompany me to her favorite shopping city in the world.

One evening we were invited for dinner by *Chiefs'* Executive Producer Bill Deneen to his spectacular apartment on swanky Park Avenue. The place was extravagantly decorated with lush silk draperies that framed sweeping views of Central Park. The long dining table was formally set with intricately carved silver serving pieces and candlesticks. Crystal stemware, designed to hold every conceivable beverage, was carefully arranged at each place setting.

We dined with another couple, guests who were also enjoying course after course of gourmet cuisine and entertaining conversation.

With a little wave to the server in the corner of the room, Bill announced that it was time for dessert. Suddenly a large platter with a silver dome was placed before me. *Wow, this is some dessert,* I thought as I waited for everyone else to be served.

"Go ahead and get started, Jerry," urged Bill with a big grin.

"That's all right. I'll wait for everyone else," I responded, not wanting to be rude, especially at such a formal dinner.

"Oh, no. I insist!" he said playfully. "This is a special dessert just for you."

Curious, I complied and lifted the heavy lid. To my astonishment, my "dessert" was a massive pile of hundred dollar bills! Marilynn and I exchange stunned glances.

Waaay off on my guess of Baked Alaska.

"We really appreciate the great job you did for us, and we wanted you to know it," he beamed.

This most enchanting evening went late into the night, but came to a rather sobering end when Marilynn and I, preparing to leave, began to realize that we had all those $100 bills to escort back with us.

With only eight blocks between our place and Bill's apartment, we had enjoyed the early evening stroll over to his apartment before dinner. But at 1:00 a.m. on the streets of New York City with all those new little friends to chaperon safely home, those eight blocks might as well have been eight hundred miles!

Suddenly very grateful for the heavy coats the autumn chill demanded, we began stuffing bills in pockets, in loose seams, down trousers, down socks, in her bra, everywhere! The shivers I felt walking down the street that night weren't from the nip in the air but from fear of what could lurk around the next corner. I wasn't about to make some mugger *that* happy!

Thankfully, Marilynn, all our paper companions, and I made it back to our place safely that night.

EXECUTIVE PRODUCING

Capitalizing on my credibility with CBS, I embarked on my first television movie for my own production company, *With Intent to Kill*. The story, a murder mystery that was shot on location in Dallas, starred Academy Award winners Karl Malden and Holly Hunter, Paul Sorvino, and William Devane. With me in the role of executive producer, this project was the directorial debut of Mike Robe, the writer of this excellent script. Mike was a sharp guy who had directed some shorts, but this was his first full-length TV film.

I also filmed three other television movies for my company: *Kiss Shot*, which starred Whoopi Goldberg, *Family Sins,* starring James Farentino, and *Manhunt for Claude Dallas*, starring Rip Torn and Matt Salinger, the son of J.D. Salinger, author of *Catcher in the Rye*.

As a side note, I also cast a beautiful unknown ingénue, Annette Bening, in her first role in *Claude Dallas*. I just knew she would go on to be a big star.

I PLEDGE ALLEGIANCE . . .

Ellis Island

A fantastic story about the struggles of the many immigrants arriving in the United States during the nineteenth century, *Ellis Island* had a blockbuster cast starring some of the greatest performers to ever step in front of a camera: Sir Richard Burton, Academy Award winner Faye Dunaway, Ben Vereen, Natasha Richardson, Melba Moore, and the list goes on and on. Oh, yeah, and a new guy . . . Liam Neeson.

The script was a brilliant piece that interwove the compelling stories of several brave immigrants as they went about making new lives in America. Some dazzling musical numbers were tossed in for good measure.

As you can imagine, with such a celebrated cast some pretty interesting stories unfolded off camera, as well.

161

The legendary Faye Dunaway is a charming and socially gracious lady. On set, she really likes to take charge—she does her own makeup, requires strict wardrobe approval, etc.

Up early and anxious to get started on first day of filming, we spent a good chunk of time prepping and lighting the set. With seventy-six-year-old Oscar Award winner for *Bridge on the River Kwai* Jack Hildyard at the helm as Director of Photography, this was sure to be a spectacular-looking production.

But it seems Ms. Dunaway had some ideas of her own.

Just before we were ready to start rolling, she appeared with a handheld mirror and walked all over the just-lit set checking herself in the mirror at each and every one of her marks.

When she had finished, she strolled up to our illustrious DP with a big smile and eyelashes fluttering. "Jaaaack," she purred, "you know I'd really look better if you would put the light right underneath the camera."

As she sauntered off, I could practically see smoke coming out of the old man's nose and ears! I darted over to him to try to douse the flames. "Hey, Jack, it's the first day of shooting. Just give her what she wants, and we'll see how it goes," I said, attempting to console the veteran. "Let's not get into anything so soon."

Jack, no stranger to actors' egos, resigned himself to the wisdom of just getting on with things and went about changing all the lighting.

The next day, I took a look at the dailies and, yes, Miss Dunaway had succeeded in making herself look "better," all right. But she had also succeeded in making herself look quite literally too young for the part!

After giving this some thought, I wandered over to see her after lunch the next day.

"Oh, hi, Jerry," she said. "Have you looked at the dailies from yesterday yet?"

"Sure have," I replied. "And we've got a problem."

"Well, what is the matter?" she asked, surprised.

"Frankly, Faye, you just look too young for the part. I don't know what we're going to do about it." Then I turned around and walked back to my chair.

As her surprise turned to shock, she scrambled over to me. I busily pretended to focus on the next setup.

"What do you mean, Jerry?" she asked, trying to contain her alarm. "What are we going to do?"

"Well, there's only one thing we can do," I said, letting my words hang in the air before continuing. "Let's drop the mirror and concentrate on the acting."

We parted with laughter, but I never had another issue with her.

I think my advice was well-placed, since she went home with the Golden Globe for her performance that year.

Faye Dunaway and Jerry

Jerry and the *Ellis Island* dancers

Once in a great while, I will run into an actor who thinks they are the director in that defiant "I know my character better than you do" sort of way.

In the role of Jacob Rubenstein—the Irving Berlin-type character—actor Peter Reigert was to lead the singing in the full-on flag-waving, red-white-and-blue, Statue of Liberty-dramatic version of "God Bless America" at the climactic end of the film. The only problem was that Peter had decided his character ". . . didn't want to sing that song because he was still a Jewish immigrant in his heart." Based on that, he flatly refused to participate.

Okaaay.

This was not exactly a scene I could omit, and nothing I said could convince him that this was the way the story was written and that he needed to play the character the way it was written in the script.

After an aggravating ordeal, I finally got him to compromise (thanks again, psychology classes) and sing just the first two lines. I was able to shoot and edit around his obstinacy and get the poignant ending I needed.

Ellis Island also brought me the lamentable privilege of directing film legend Richard Burton in his last-ever performance. He struggled to remember his lines, so his ever-present script was always in hand, making it very clear how much the alcohol had taken its toll on him. While still engaging, his performance was largely patched together in the editing room.

He was, however, one of the nicest men in the world. We spent a good deal of time together on set chatting away between takes while waiting for lighting, etc. Without fail, his favorite topic was Elizabeth Taylor. In spite of the fact he had been married to another woman for a good number of years, he never stopped talking about Elizabeth: the two-million-dollar diamond he had bought her, how they'd met on the set of Cleopatra, and on and on. His stories left me with the strong impression there was still a love there that no number of divorces could ever end or time could ever extinguish.

About three weeks after he had finished his part, word came to the set that Richard had suffered a fatal stroke. Making his loss all the more poignant was that his daughter Kate Burton was also in the cast and their scenes together as father and daughter were deeply moving, even without any inkling of Richard's impending fate. Kate returned to the set after attending her father's funeral to a sea of heavy hearts.

Kate Burton, Richard Burton, and Jerry

TOO MANY BOOBS ON THE BEACH

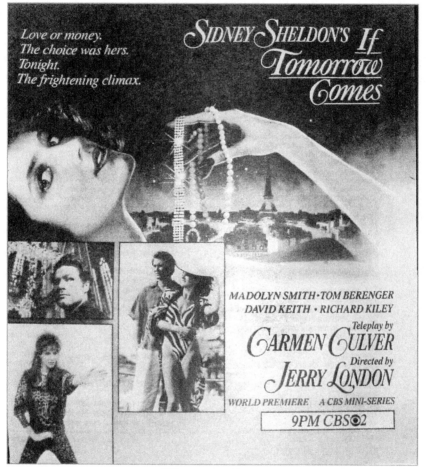

If Tomorrow Comes

The bestseller penned by Sydney Sheldon, *If Tomorrow Comes*, was prime miniseries material, and I couldn't wait to do it.

Our screen adaption became a seven-hour drama starring Tom Berenger and Madolyn Smith, along with the original Don Quixote in *Man of La Mancha*, Richard Kiley. It was also the second time I cast the up-and-coming Liam Neeson.

Stunning locations made the shoot that much more enticing: L.A., New Orleans, Amsterdam, Cannes, Italy, and finishing off in London. By far, this was the best itinerary I'd had the pleasure to shoot.

Foreign destinations can be intoxicating costars, but every once in a while the flavor these locations lend can be a little too exotic for American tastes.

Such was the case on a bright, beautiful day on the golden sands of France's Côte d'Azur in Cannes as we were setting up a shot with Tom and Madolyn. With the hundreds of extras on the beach finally wrangled into place, we started rolling.

"Cuuut!" I shouted.

My French first AD darted over to see what the problem was.

"We can't shoot this!" I protested. "Look at the extras on the beach. Every one of the women is topless. I'm looking at a sea of tits!"

"So?" he said, shrugging his shoulders. "This is France."

"This may very well be France, but I'm shooting this for American television," I said emphatically. "Tell them to put their tops back on."

A look of horror flooded his face. "I'm not going to tell them to put their tops back on!" he snapped indignantly. "I am French! YOU tell them!" He huffed off.

When I stopped laughing, I stepped to the front of the set and said, "Ladies, for this scene we ask that you please put your tops on," even though a part of me wished I were French, too!

Is Italian Roadkill on the Menu?

While happily free to pursue my passion for minis, and ever on the lookout for a great script, I somehow always ended up directing "one more" pilot for CAA's darling, Aaron Spelling.

One of them being a pilot called *Hollywood Beat*, which starred Jack Scalia. While the show was maybe not exactly memorable to the public—it only lasted for one season—it was certainly memorable to me. I shot an episode that, along with the additional pleasure of working with guest star Robert Englund aka Freddy Krueger from *Nightmare on Elm Street* fame, will remain forever etched in my mind.

We were shooting a car crash stunt at Hollywood Boulevard and Las Palmas Avenue, right around the corner from our next location inside of Miceli's, the oldest Italian restaurant in Hollywood. This landmark is where they'd filmed Lucy tossing her pizza crust in one episode of *I Love Lucy*. It was a favorite hangout of Frank, Dean, DiMaggio, Presidents Nixon and Kennedy, The Beatles, and many others.

A special location, indeed.

A ton of preparation goes into shooting a dangerous stunt—especially in the middle of Hollywood. But in spite of all the security, crowd control, streets being shut down and taped off, production assistants wrangling extras, and a car barreling down the street at full speed for the big crash, an elderly gentleman still managed to suddenly step off the curb into the street—right in front of the speeding car!

John Moio, my sharp-as-a-tack stunt coordinator, had the presence of mind to leap out and tackle the guy. The two men went flying, landing on the pavement. Thanks to John, the old gent avoided becoming roadkill as the car missed him by inches!

We all stood frozen, stunned at what we had just seen.

Well. Gratitude for literally having spared this guy a one-way ticket to the morgue was not on this old man's mind as he was helped to his feet. He was not happy to be alive. He was just mad as hell!

Seemingly oblivious of his narrow escape, he carried on swearing and cussing out his savior for his brutish behavior as he stormed off across the street and right through the front door of Miceli's.

Yep, it just so happened that Mr. Carmen Miceli had been crossing the street on his way to work that day at his Hollywood landmark.

To say that Mr. Miceli was no longer enamored with having the film crew that had almost rolled him flatter than a pepperoni pizza in to shoot their next scene at his restaurant could be in the running for one of the understatements of all time.

With the day's schedule now in serious jeopardy, and not quite sure how to back my way out of someone else's near-death experience, I looked around for reinforcement. Duke Vincent, Aaron Spelling's longtime partner who had been on the set to see the big stunt that day, now hurried into the restaurant to see what he could do to salvage the shoot.

Seems sharing Italian blood—and a glass of wine or two, or five—can go a long way toward smoothing over the rough edges of having nearly become a hood ornament for a speeding Chevy.

With the green light to film inside the restaurant restored, we quickly went about setting up our next shot.

Duke tossed us a wink on his way out the door, as Carmen Miceli stood by waving *ciao* to his new best friend.

Liam Who?

A little closer to home, I directed a movie called *Dark Mansions*. It was a tale of a young woman's journey to a creepy estate after being hired to write the matriarch owner's memoirs, only to have things go awry when she discovers she's the spitting image of a long-dead ancestor. It starred Hollywood legend Miss Joan Fontaine, Linda Purl, and playing the male lead, Michael York.

Nothing against Mr. York, who is a very fine British actor, but he wasn't my first choice for the lead in this role. I had cast a young, unknown actor in a couple of earlier projects, whose work I was extremely taken with and who was just perfect for this role.

Aaron Spelling, however, was dead set on Michael York.

"C'mon, Aaron, this guy is great," I said. "You've probably never seen him, so let me get some tape to you."

"Fine, Jerry, I'm happy to take a look, and I'll consider him if I see any talent there."

So I collected some tape from small parts I had cast him in, got it edited, and brought it over to Aaron. "What do you think? Pretty great, huh?" I boasted, knowing I had just brought this brilliant unknown talent to the attention of Mr. Aaron Spelling.

"I don't think the audience will relate to him," Aaron scowled. "His accent's not right or something. I just don't see it."

That was the end of that, and we went with Michael York.

Who was the new actor I was so crazy about?

A guy by the name of Liam Neeson.

Jerry, Liam Neeson, and Alice Krige

LIZA, BURT, AND A BAD SCRIPT

By now you might be wondering why I didn't pursue a transition to feature films. I could list hundreds of reasons this didn't happen. Topping the list would be my highest priority—quality scripts. Then, of course, there was the fact that CAA was keeping me otherwise busy cranking out Spelling pilots.

But when I was asked to direct the comedy feature film *Rent-a-Cop*, which starred mega-star Burt Reynolds, obviously I agreed.

The first director of *Rent-a-Cop*, a cop-falls-for-prostitute comedy, had dropped out, which should have been my first clue. The script was weak, but I was (of course) promised a rewrite, so I signed on to do it. Having had enough "script rewrite" promises broken in the past, you'd think I would have known better by then. I guess some of us are either blind optimists or just slow learners.

The female lead went to the irrepressible Liza Minnelli, who was a delight to work with. She even agreed to call my daughter Lisa from the set to wish her a happy birthday, and ended up singing her own little rendition of "Happy Birthday to You" on the phone! A real sweetheart, to be sure.

After the smashing success of the *Smokey And the Bandit* franchise and massive hits such as *The Longest Yard* and *Best Little Whorehouse in Texas*, not to mention the nude centerfold spread in *Cosmopolitan* magazine, Burt Reynolds was as hot as they came.

Burt had also tried his hand at directing (*The End* and *Sharky's Machine*), but by the late '80s, the heat on him had begun to cool.

Maybe it was the unfulfilled promises for rewrites, or maybe it was something else entirely, but ultimately directing Burt's ego was a serious challenge. Every time I would try to address some of the more anemic lines in the script with him, I was reminded that it was he who had been the top box office draw for four straight years, so who was *I* to tell *him* what was funny? We were clearly not working as a team.

Should'a listened to my instincts.

So be it. The net results of the film tell the true story.

Rent-a-Cop—Burt Reynolds, Liza Minelli, and Jerry

FAMILY SINS

Not that I need to repeat that I believe a good script is the sole backbone of any quality film, but I once saw this illustrated in a particularly odd way.

I had been playing tennis one day with a fellow I didn't know well. Over the postgame iced tea cooldown, the predictable "what do you do?" banter ensued. Turns out this man was a child psychologist, who began sharing some pretty fascinating case histories. Particularly intriguing was an especially disturbing case of infanticide, a sibling murder with the mother taking the blame to save the living child.

With shades of Bobby Small and his hotel stories echoing in my head, I asked the psychologist if it would be possible for me to take a look at the case to see if I could do anything with it. He agreed.

So I got a writer and created a script, which I took in to CBS where I had my production deal. I was instantly met with, "It's a great script, but we cannot possibly do anything this dark."

And that was that.

Four years later, I got a call from CBS. "Jerry, remember that script you had about infanticide? I think we're changing the kind of films we do here and we'd really like to take another look at it."

Six weeks later, we were in production on *Family Sins*, starring James Farentino and Jill Eikenberry.

Proof that a good script truly has a life of its own.

My Midnight Express

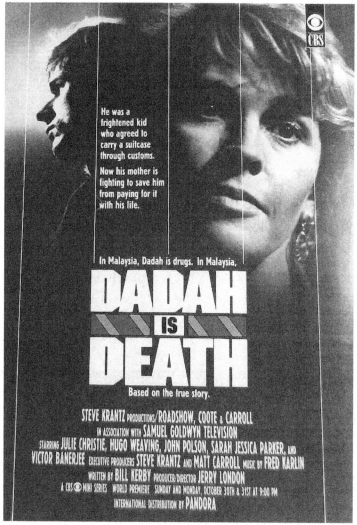

He was a frightened kid who agreed to carry a suitcase through customs.

Now his mother is fighting to save him from paying for it with his life.

In Malaysia, Dadah is drugs. In Malaysia,

DADAH IS DEATH

Based on the true story.

STEVE KRANTZ PRODUCTIONS/ROADSHOW, COOTE & CARROLL
IN ASSOCIATION WITH SAMUEL GOLDWYN TELEVISION
STARRING JULIE CHRISTIE, HUGO WEAVING, JOHN POLSON, SARAH JESSICA PARKER, AND
VICTOR BANERJEE EXECUTIVE PRODUCERS STEVE KRANTZ AND MATT CARROLL MUSIC BY FRED KARLIN
WRITTEN BY BILL KERBY PRODUCER/DIRECTOR JERRY LONDON
A CBS MINI SERIES WORLD PREMIERE SUNDAY AND MONDAY, OCTOBER 30TH & 31ST AT 9:00 PM
INTERNATIONAL DISTRIBUTION BY PANDORA

Dadah is Death

Sometimes difficult to deal with on a personal level, the darker topics often result in the most compelling films.

Never was this more true than when I first read the riveting script of *Dadah is Death*. It was a gut-wrenching true story of Australian mother Barbara Barlow embarking on a monumental worldwide crusade to save her son's life after he and his friend were sentenced to hanging for smuggling heroin in a Malaysian airport where signs had recently been posted: Dadah is Death.

I was reminded of the same tension in my favorite film *Midnight Express*, and knew I just had to do it.

Barbara Barlow went to the highest levels of authority, with pleas to the Reagan White House, Margaret Thatcher's Parliament, even all the way to the Vatican, gripping the entire world at that time as the excruciating drama unfolded.

Academy Award winner Julie Christie in the lead role of Barbara Barlow was just fantastic to work with. One of the few lighter moments of this journey was escorting the lovely Ms. Christie to dinner on the occasion of her forty-seventh birthday. She was delightful and engaging, although I couldn't help but notice that a fair amount of our conversation revolved around a soft spot she still had for Warren Beatty.

We were shooting interiors in Sydney and exteriors in Kuala Lumpur, the latter not being exactly eager to roll out the welcome mat for people telling the appalling truth to the whole world.

Consequently, when my art director Ro Bruen-Cook, DP Julian Penney, and I landed in Kuala Lumpur to scout the locations, we were told in no uncertain terms that we were not welcome. We decided to "explore the sights" like tourists while surreptitiously scouting locations, then get the hell out in less than six hours. Not willing to tell this story without footage of the actual locations in which it took place—especially the prison—I decided the risk was worth taking.

I went back to Sydney to shoot the interiors while the campaign to get the Malaysian government's permission to film there continued. As we neared the completion of filming in Sydney, word came that Malaysia steadfastly refused to allow us to film. Period. Apparently, Thailand had also been enlisted to boycott our production.

I remembered my production team in Hong Kong who were instrumental in the filming of *Shōgun*, and asked them to take a look at the script to see if they could come up with suitable alternatives for some of the exteriors. Jumping on it, they were off to Macau. They got back to me with video of various locations, most of which would work.

Still, I wasn't going to compromise on ground zero of this story—the prison where these kids had been executed. That place *had* to appear in this film. Again relying on my well-placed connections in Asia, I contacted a director of photography, a Malaysian national who was willing to go out and get the prison footage I needed to knit the film together.

While busy filming in Macau one day, I learned that he had been confronted by the police outside the prison in Kuala Lumpur where he'd been filming for us. To throw them off, he shrewdly insisted he was just shooting a commercial. But the police, having none of it, arrested him and his small crew. Given the grim realities of the horrendous event I had been immersing myself in with the telling of the *Dadah* story, my heart practically stopped when I heard this.

I don't quite know how—possibly because of his citizenship—but he managed to get released pretty quickly. God only knows the peril he put himself into *again* when he actually went back to the prison to get our footage. Within hours of being released, he finagled his way up to the highest rooftop near the prison to nail that shot!

In spite of the horrific subject matter, I am very proud of the film, and I am particularly grateful for Barbara Barlow's blessing and participation in helping us tell her tale of unimaginable tragedy.

I was lucky enough to have my friend, Emmy-winning editor Michael Brown, edit this mini for me.

JERRY LONDON

MAKIN' WHOOPI

As television began to expand its programming to include darker material, there were still lighter offerings on the agenda.

Kiss Shot was a script we developed for a Movie of the Week for CBS, which followed in the footsteps of the smash feature film, *The Color of Money*. While still in development, we heard that Whoopi Goldberg was looking for something to do, so I had the writer make a few changes.

The lead pool shark, originally a man, was now a woman and a divorced mom who needed to make quick cash shooting pool. Opposite Whoopi starred the ever-popular Dennis Franz of *Hill Street Blues* fame.

Casting Whoopi was a great move, not only because she was one of the funniest people I'd ever worked with or because the mood was always "up" on set when she was around, but because the syndication rights doubled overnight due to her participation.

With a mouth that made Suzanne Pleshette sound like a girl scout, Whoopi had us in stitches most of the time. Everyone adored her.

"Jerry, I can't do these lines," she moaned on the set one day.

"Whaat?" I paused. "What's wrong with 'em, Whoopi?"

"They're just wrong. Don't make me do them. I'd rather go down and blow you," she cracked.

We all busted up!

She was a hard worker, too. As she really needed to be able to handle a cue stick to make this project work, I hired the top pool instructor in the United States to train with her. She practiced day and night, until she was ripping off trick shots like an old pro.

If the day was going to run a bit longer than planned, all we had to do was have a production assistant wander down to the local antique shops Whoopi had been scouting for her glassware collection, and pick out a piece she'd been coveting.

Sometimes it doesn't take much to make an actor happy. The thoughtfulness of a little trinket can go a long way.

Jerry and Whoopi Goldberg

Don't Ask—This is Italy!

A Season of Giants

A fter the success of *The Scarlet and The Black*, I was a rock star in Italy. One Italian production company in particular was after me to come do a film there.

It's important to note here that when I did *The Scarlet and The Black*, it was shot in Italy; however, the company in charge of the production was American.

When this next project in Italy came along, I was more than happy to take a long look at it.

A Season of Giants was an artistically brilliant adventure about the early life of Michelangelo that saw him along with other artistic geniuses, including Da Vinci, Raphael, and the Medicis, navigating their various rivalries and alliances as they faced the religious and political turmoil of their time.

The stumbling point was that it was written by Italians, and then translated to English. Let's just say it didn't translate well, and ended up coming off more like an interesting and detailed art history lesson than a compelling and dramatic film. It simply lacked the drama needed to sustain its six-hour length. The script wasn't great, but it was going to be done in Italy for Italians, so I figured what the heck. Only later did I learn that TNT bought the domestic rights and wanted it cut down to four hours for airing in the United States.

I loved working in Italy, plus I'd have my fantastic assistant director Gianni Cozzo, who worked with me on *The Scarlet and The Black,* by my side, so I was set to go.

We had the brilliant actor F. Murray Abraham signed on as Pope Julius II, but the hunt for our Michelangelo was a noteworthy experience. Being an Italian production, most of the talent was Italian; however, most of the leads were British, so I found myself in London casting alongside the famous British casting director, Rose Tobias Shaw.

After interviewing dozens of actors in a London studio, Rose and I ventured out to a play one night to see Mark Frankel, a talented, sensitive, good-looking kid of about twenty-five. Rose gave her stamp of approval and Mark was in.

He did a terrific job in the role of Michelangelo. It was no small feat to take on the role of one the greatest artists of all time. Sadly, I heard a couple of years later that he had been killed in a motorcycle accident, cutting short the life of an extremely talented actor. What a loss.

In spite of the fact that we had an eleven-million-dollar budget on this project—a healthy sum in those days—we needed every last dime of it to recreate such treasures as Michelangelo's David and a little place called the Sistine Chapel. Having been fortunate enough to get a private tour alone at night with the curator of the Sistine Chapel, I was highly motivated to get this right. The tour truly was a soul-stirring religious experience . . . and that's really saying something for this Jewish boy!

Two weeks ahead of shooting, Gianni dropped a little bomb on me. "Hey Jerry, the word just came down from the Italians that we are over budget, and they have to cut it," he said.

"We haven't even started to shoot yet. What do you mean, cut it?" I asked, confused.

"Yeah, they cut the budget to nine million," he said matter-of-factly.

"Wait a minute. You mean they're cutting two million out of the budget? That's nuts!" I protested. "We're gonna have to cut pages and pages! We're gonna have to condense scenes! The art in this project *has* to be first rate!"

Gianni didn't react.

"So, where did that money go?" I pressed. I really wanted to know what the hell could've happened to all that money this close to shooting.

"Don't ask," he said quietly. "This is Italy."

It seems one thing I didn't know about working in Italy was the considerable sums required to grease the wheels of production. In this case, apparently one million dollars had gone to the RAI network, and another million straight into the pocket of the executive producer. The exec producer was a tall, imposing fellow who wore a long black coat and a large diamond ring on his finger, and had a Godfather-like penchant for extending his hand so new acquaintances could kiss his ring.

About halfway through filming, I was handed three new scenes. Reading them over, I noticed that each of them had one woman in it. Three different scenes, three different women. Not only did these scenes have nothing to do with each other, they had nothing whatsoever to do with the script!

"What's going on?" I ask Gianni after reading the scenes.

"The producers would like these actresses to be in your movie," he said as diplomatically as he could.

"Well, can I meet them?" I asked, still puzzled.

"Oh, sure, we can do that," he said.

The following day I carved out an hour of time for appointments at the production office to meet with the three actresses. What I met with instead were three incensed women who could not comprehend why they had to read anything, since they already had the parts!

Three lampposts propped against a cardboard box could have done a better reading than these women, but you knew that was coming, now, didn't you?

"I can't shoot these scenes, Gianni. They're garbage!" I protested in a last-ditch effort to spare myself a colossal waste of time.

"Look Jerry, this is Italy. Just shoot them," he replied calmly. "Don't worry about it, you can just take care of them in editing."

Damned straight I will.

The six-hour shoot took me about four months. I really didn't want to stay in Italy any longer than that, so part of my deal had been that I would take the film home with me and do the editing in the U.S.

Upon completion of filming, I headed back to the States, not really concerned that the production company still owed me my last payment, because I still had four weeks of editing left to do.

Weeks later, I finally finished my final cut—*sans* the three cardboard bimbos—and got it ready to ship. Still no paycheck, which by this time warranted a call to my business manager. He assured me he would write the production offices in Italy and get the situation taken care of.

Four *more* weeks passed, and still no response from Italy.

"Look, just take the film, box it up, put it in the vault, and don't do anything until we hear from them," my attorney advised. Finding no fault with that strategy, I set about packing the film for storage and closing up the editing office.

Two weeks later I got a call from my business manager. The check had finally arrived. It contained no response to his letter, no apology, no nothing. Just a check in the full amount owed.

Great. So I got the film out, prepped it, and shipped it off to Rome.

The very next morning I was startled awake by a 6:00 a.m. phone call. "Meester London, dis isa de Bank de Italia," came the voice at the other end.

"Yes?" croaked my early-morning voice.

"Yastudaya we send a money order drafta to you accounta. We should not a senda you disa money." The heavy Italian accent echoed on the line. "We senda by a mistake, so woulda you please returna de money?"

I literally had to put my hand over the receiver to hide my laughter. "Well, listen," I said, trying hard to disguise the amusement in my voice, "I don't have anything to do with handling the money. You're going to have to go through my business manager."

I then called my business manager, who assured me that another letter would be promptly sent to the Italian production company, clarifying the accounting and notifying them that we were in receipt of the final payment, thus satisfying and closing out our financial dealings with them.

The next communication I had from Italy had nothing to do with the accidental payment of my salary. Rather, it was a demand to know where the three missing scenes were, and orders to put them back in!

Umm . . . No.

I explained that I would be happy to send the deleted scenes to them, which they were most welcome to put into the Italian version, but that I would handle the American cut here.

Ultimately, in spite of the fact that the American version was edited down to four hours and was visually striking, to my mind it still didn't overcome its lack of drama. In any case, it was well received here.

But this story doesn't end here.

Three years later, my son Todd—a very successful producer in his own right—received a letter addressed to me. In it, I found a subpoena to appear in the Italian court for a lawsuit brought by The Bank of Italia for not returning my last paycheck to them!

In spite of being assured by my business manager and various attorneys that all had been sorted out, still for the next ten years I never stepped foot in Italy! This drove my Italy-loving wife nuts! But I can assure you that being arrested and tossed into an Italian prison for God-knows-how-long was never high on my bucket list!

Not long after this episode, Marilynn and I were on a visit to San Francisco, enjoying a lovely dinner with good friends Tony and Lucille Sanchez-Corea, who are delightful people and the parents of my daughter's sorority sister. Given Tony's rather unusual and fascinating employment history and serious familiarity with Italy, my rather aberrant Italian adventures were a perfect topic for dinnertime conversation.

"Hmm, why don't I take a look into it, Jerry?" Tony offered while pouring another glass of wine. "See if I can find anything out for you."

For a large majority of the population, this would have been a polite offer at best, but coming from Tony, it carried some serious weight.

Did I mention that Tony had worked for the Vatican??

Yep, as the attaché to the Vatican, in the Knights of Malta, no less. Tony and Lucille had lived and worked in Italy for four years in their *apartamento* near St. Peter's Square. If Tony says he can check something out in Italy, he can check something out in Italy.

He simply contacted his friend, the Monsignor Orgolini who, naturally with access to just about anything he wanted to know, sorted through government files until, *mamma mia*, my name was nowhere to be found on any "wanted" list in Italy!

All my wife heard was, "We're cleared for take-off!"

I DON'T DO NUDE

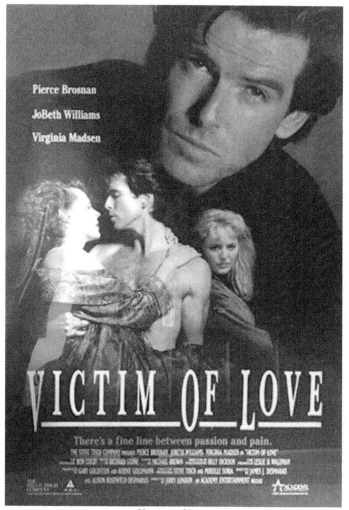

Victim of Love

A long with the aforementioned swing toward darker tales, nothing illustrated television's simultaneous move to more adult content better than the sexy thriller I directed called *Victim of Love*, starring Virginia

Madsen and Pierce Brosnan, a future James Bond. It was basically a softcore porn script that had been cleaned up for television.

I fought the network for Virginia, who was essentially unknown at the time, but who possessed that great sexy quality that reads so well on film. I just knew she was perfect for the part. The screen lit up with the electric chemistry between Pierce and Virginia.

The only objection Virginia ever raised was a reticence to do any nudity. I assured her before we ever started that nudity wasn't even an option by reminding her that this was an American TV movie. The irony of that conversation gave me a chuckle on set one day when shooting the couple in the first bedroom scene, to find Virginia clad in nothing more than a—shall we say—sheer, nothing-left-to-the-imagination negligee.

Needless to say, I had to call wardrobe in to make some ready-for-primetime adjustments!

Y'ALL DON'T COME BACK NOW, Y'HEAR?

A nother tale from the South, this time the topic being politics, sort of picking up where *Chiefs* left off, was written by Stuart Woods. *Grass Roots* was a four-hour miniseries starring Claude Akins, Raymond Burr, and Joanna Cassidy.

You never know what little idiosyncrasies actors may present while on a set. I was met with one such surprise when a setup called for Raymond Burr to drive a golf cart into the scene.

"Are you kidding me?" The actor was aghast. "I don't drive!"

All the assurances in the world to Mr. Burr that driving a golf cart was absolutely nothing like driving a car simply fell on deaf ears. He steadfastly refused to drive the golf cart. We shot the scene with the cart parked. Nevertheless, Mr. Burr was a very polished actor and a real pleasure to work with.

We had had such a fantastic, warm, welcoming, and wonderful experience with our host town of Chester in South Carolina for the long *Chiefs* shoot that I couldn't wait to enjoy the South again. This adventure, however, unfolded a little differently. I got to observe firsthand how even that warm Southern hospitality has its limits.

And rightfully so.

After a night of letting off perhaps a bit too much steam, it seems our lead actor's makeup artist got herself tossed into the slammer, and she would be—to put it lightly—unavailable for work the following day.

Well, for whatever reason, this really set our actor off. He launched into a loud tirade about how he "hated this fucking town," and "how the hell can you stupid rednecks do this?" and on and on. Something one might want to carefully reconsider doing while standing on a huge set filled with hardworking Southern teamsters who are, as likely as not, packing heat. But, no. On and on he raged about the "dumb Southern sons of bitches" and how much he hated this place, until he finally sat down on the floor right in the middle of the set in his own personal protest, refusing to work until his makeup artist was set free.

I strolled over to where he sat to quietly assure him that I was sure she'd be out soon and to suggest we just get a couple of shots done in the meantime.

Nope. He was having none of it. He refused to work until she was out.

In the course of precariously negotiating to get both the makeup artist released and this actor back to work, I finally managed to get him to cooperate.

At last settling back to the business at hand of setting up the next shot, my assistant director suddenly motioned me aside. "Hey Jerry, I don't know if it's true or not," he said, glancing over his shoulder, "but I'm hearing rumblings on the set. A few of the guys are planning to follow him home tonight and 'take care of him.'"

Oh, crap.

"Okay. Well, whatever you do, *do not* let this get back to the actor," I stressed.

He didn't.

The third assistant director did.

Next thing you know, there was our bad boy actor handing a small wad of cash over to his assistant with instructions to go out and buy him a pistol.

Thinking this wasn't looking to end well, I lingered around the set after we had wrapped for the day to see if this was going to go anyplace or if it was just a bunch of overblown, testosterone-driven saber rattling.

I was actively praying for the latter, as shooting actors from hospital beds or jail cells wasn't an option.

I watched the actor get into his car with his driver. Then I saw two other cars loaded with crew following him out.

Jumping straight into my car, I instructed the driver to follow them.

The cars full of crew followed the actor to the front of his hotel. Watching from a distance, I saw him get out and head toward the entrance. A couple of the guys in the other cars stepped out and made damned sure their presence was known by the actor before he rushed into his hotel.

While he may have seemed a bit edgier than usual on the set following this little escapade, the intimidation seemed to work. Mr. Mouth finished the show quietly.

Months later, I was watching Mr. Badass-Wanna-Be promoting the upcoming miniseries on NBC's *The Tonight Show* with Johnny Carson.

"Hey, I heard you shot the movie down South. How did you like it there?" Johnny innocently inquired.

"I hated it, and I'll never go back!" he mouthed off. "What a bunch of rednecks!" And off he went—again.

This time the insulted audience was not a bunch of crew members standing on a set in Georgia, but the entire South! With the whole country watching!

The fallout out was huge. The newspapers in Atlanta went nuts and set about instigating a full-on boycott of the show. They were pretty successful, too. The ratings throughout the entire South were nonexistent.

His blowout proved costly to both the actor and NBC. He didn't work for quite a while after that incident.

Guess you could say his career went "South."

THE COS

I first worked with Bill Cosby when I shot *I Spy* in the wonderful city of Vienna, Austria. The script had originally called for Rome, but with plenty of experience shooting in Italy, I knew we could not accomplish what was called for in this script on the streets of Rome. I suggested Vienna, everyone agreed, and it worked out just beautifully.

Apparently Mr. Cosby enjoyed the shoot as much as I did, because shortly afterward when he was preparing a pilot for NBC called *The Cosby Mystery Movies*, he asked me to direct.

Bill Cosby and Jerry

My experiences with Mr. Cosby were not only of a prepared professional actor, but of a generous man. It was commonplace for him to show up with doughnuts, bagels, or some other kind of treat for the entire crew.

We shot the pilot episode for the *Cosby Mystery Movies* in New York City, where I just love to shoot. The gritty streets and perpetual energy of that city always provide a spectacular backdrop on film to any action or dialogue.

Shooting Bill crossing Columbus Avenue one day, a woman who recognized him jumped out of nowhere right into the shot to greet him with a handshake. In spite of the fact that it totally ruined the shot, he finished chatting with his fan, who eventually went on her way with no idea of her intrusion.

One day in particular perfectly illustrates the man I worked with.

I was figuring out a scene on the streets using a Steadicam with a locally hired camera operator. As I explained to him what I was after in the scene, I was continually rebuffed with reasons why none of it could be done, all delivered in a defiant, barking tone.

Apparently overhearing the conversation, Bill suddenly stepped in. "Young man, could I speak with you for a second?" He took the disgruntled cameraman aside. "The director is the commander on the set, and we don't show disrespect to the commander," he said at full volume, staring the operator right in the eyes, "and I think you should apologize to him."

Needless to say, I got exactly the shots I wanted. That just shows you the kind of man Bill was to work with.

QUINN, WILLIE, AND DOLLY . . . AND BEYOND

As the 1980s wound down, so did the miniseries format. The minis largely disappeared from non-subscription television. The cable network explosion would provide the new outlet for the long-form format.

I busied myself closer to home with movies and TV series. *Dr. Quinn, Medicine Woman* was one such show. It was a period western, shot locally in Los Angeles at the historic Paramount Ranch near Malibu. I thoroughly enjoyed that show, and shot over twenty episodes in the six years it ran. Jane Seymour and Joe Lando's professionalism of always being prepared, combined with Creator/Producer Beth Sullivan's first-rate scripts and trust in my process, made this close to the top in my list of favorite series I directed.

The cast of *Dr. Quinn*

197

We had a diverse parade of guest stars on that show. One of my all-time favorites was Willie Nelson and his traveling Black Mariah trailer. Even though I never once saw him smoking, whenever I'd step inside that ol' black Mariah of his to chat about an upcoming scene, I swear I would step out high as a kite from residual fumes!

Willie Nelson and Jerry

I came full circle in a funny way on one movie I did called *The Barbara Mandrell Story*, because it starred Maureen McCormick, with whom I had worked (Marsha Brady) on *The Brady Bunch*. It also starred the ebullient Dolly Parton, whom I thoroughly enjoyed working with. Dolly, I learned, does not fly, so she drove her trailer to every location. Her trailer smelled like flowers and perfume. As soon as you meet her, you love her!

Jerry and Dolly

Never one to shy away from an interesting location shoot, I was delighted to take the helm of a movie called *Counter Strike*, which was a story about terrorism aboard the *QE2*. I got to work with my daughter Lisa, a successful casting director in her own right, who did the casting for that film. There were shoots scheduled in Australia, as well as a week at sea aboard the *QE2* to get the footage we needed onboard ship. This perk went over nicely at home, thank you very much.

Before you start wondering if this guy will ever learn his lesson . . . I did my homework and learned that the sheer size of the *QE2* made it one of the most stable vessels at sea; thus, motion sickness was rarely ever a problem, so I was covered. All the same, I made sure to stuff plenty of Bonine in my suitcase!

For whatever reason, at the last minute the *QE2* shipping line, Cunard, backed out of the deal, refusing to let us shoot onboard the ship. So we built a massive, and I mean *massive*, superstructure of the ship on a huge lot in Los Angeles, which served as a "stand in" for some of the shots on the decks. The rest of the shots were done digitally. In the end, of course, it all came together beautifully, thanks to the magic of skillful editing and computer-generated images.

I finagled my way to New York to direct a series, *100 Centre Street*, with its producer Sidney Lumet, the Academy Award-winning writer and director of films such as *Serpico, Prince of the City*, and *Network*.

Jerry and Academy Award-winning Writer/Director/Producer Sidney Lumet

This series was the first to be shot on location with digital cameras and filmed like live television. It was like shooting a multiple camera show, but you could see immediately what you had shot and could adjust the angles and performances on the spot. It starred Academy Award winner Alan Arkin, a real pro, and a pretty bit player named Kerry Washington, who would later star in the TV series *Scandal*.

ON TO THE NEXT SCENE

Movies and television inform us, make us laugh, make us cry, and, above all else, make us think. They provide a common experience in an increasingly divided world.

Filmmaking is nothing if not the epitome of teamwork. When a director calls out the word, "Action!" it triggers a vast, integrated, highly organized system to kick into gear in order to capture that moment on film. That single word is often glamorized in the minds of movie buffs, but what would a director's call of "Action!" be without the cinematographers, lighting techs, set designers, sound engineers, grips, electricians, assistants, and countless other individuals devoted to creating excellence in entertainment upon that command? Nothing more than a lonely echo on an empty sound stage. I would never have enjoyed the successes I've had without the brilliant work of the men and women who labored alongside me.

Volumes will forever be written about the accomplishments of those involved in filmmaking, but there is another group of people toiling in the shadows. It is the families of those employed in the entertainment industry. For every award you see us stepping up to receive, there should be one issued to our families, as well. They bear the enormous burdens of the long separations, a child's anguish from a parent's absence at a birthday party, the double duty created by a missing spouse, the sometimes-lengthy lapses between jobs, and the occasional hurtful brush-off from those pushing to seek favor with us. They are truly the heroes that quietly support every production.

My personal reflections of my own journey would not be complete without acknowledging those who sustained me on and off the set.

Filmmaking has always been in my blood, and always will be. I will never stop creating projects or inspiring others to achieve their goals in the entertainment industry.

I have taught film production at the USC School of Cinematic Arts, the American Film School in Hollywood, and at UCLA, helping students to produce their own short films.

Opening the eyes of aspiring filmmakers to the many dynamic elements that can go overlooked in film production is extremely gratifying. Important subtle elements that contribute to the overall impact of a film, not to mention commitment, persistence, integrity, hard work, and respect for your fellow crew members cannot be overemphasized.

My career has provided me with some extremely proud moments, but none compare to my pride in my two accomplished children, who have carved out their own paths in show business.

My daughter Lisa is a successful film and television casting director, who has discovered some of the biggest stars of today.

My son Todd, now Senior Vice President of Feature Post Production at Walt Disney Studios, started as an assistant editor. He worked his way up to producer on HBO's *Rome*, and won an Emmy for the HBO miniseries, *The Pacific,* along the way.

Even the next generation of Londons is showing signs of show business DNA. My grandson Collin is an aspiring director who is writing and directing his own short films and currently working as a production assistant, and my granddaughter Savannah is learning about fashion and costume design. Certainly seems to run in this family! Only time will tell what my influence will be on my most recent grandson Keaton.

Above all else, my journey has taught me that *there is no price on integrity* and that *it pays to be fearless in the face of obstacles.*

This is show business, after all.

What could possibly go wrong?

That's a wrap.

Jerry London
Director

Miniseries:

A Season of Giants (4-hour)—F. Murray Abraham

Chiefs (6-hour, Emmy Nomination)—Charlton Heston

Dadah is Death (4-hour)—Julie Christie

Ellis Island (7-hour, Emmy Nomination)—Richard Burton, Faye Dunaway

Evening in Byzantium (4-hour)—Glenn Ford, Shirley Jones

Grass Roots (4-hour)—Claude Akins, Raymond Burr, Joanna Cassidy

If Tomorrow Comes (7-hour)—Tom Berenger

Shōgun (12-hour, DGA Award, Emmy Award)—Richard Chamberlain

The Scarlet and the Black (4-hour)—Gregory Peck, Christopher Plummer

Wheels (10-hour)—Rock Hudson, Lee Remick

Women in White (4-hour)—Patty Duke

JERRY LONDON

MOVIES FOR TELEVISION
A Mother's Gift—Nancy McKeon, Adrian Pasdar
A Promise to Carolyn—Delta Burke, Swoosie Kurtz
As Time Runs Out—Stephen Collins
Beauty—Hal Holbrook, Janine Turner
Chicago Story—Dennis Franz
Counterstrike
Father Figure—Timothy Hutton
Harry's Hong Kong—David Soul
I Spy Returns—Bill Cosby, Robert Culp
I'll Be Home for Christmas—Jack Palance, Ann Jillian
Kiss Shot—Whoopi Goldberg
Labor of Love—Ann Jillian, Tracey Gold
Manhunt for Claude Dallas—Rip Torn
Sarah Hardy—Sela Ward, Polly Bergen
Stolen Women—Janine Turner
Swan Song—David Soul
The Bambi Bembenek Story—Timothy Busfield
The Barbara Mandrell Story—Barbara Mandrell, Dolly Parton
The Cosby Mysteries—Bill Cosby
The Gift of Life—Susan Dey
The John Denver Story—Chad Lowe
The *Ordeal of Bill Carney*—Richard Crenna, Ray Sharkey
Twist of the Knife—Dick Van Dyke
Vestige of Honor—Gerald McRaney
Victim of Love—Pierce Brosnan, JoBeth Williams

PILOTS
Chicago Story
Cover Girls
Dark Mansions
Delvecchio
Escapade

Harry's Hong Kong
Hollywood Beat
Hotel
MacGruder and Loud
The Cosby Mysteries
World of Darkness

EPISODIC TELEVISION:
Baretta
Chicago Hope
Dream On
Dr. Quinn, Medicine Woman
Hogan's Heroes
Jag
Kojak
Love American Style
Marcus Welby, MD
Police Story
Rockford Files
Sidney Lumet's *100 Centre Street*
Strong Medicine
The Bob Newhart Show
The Guardian
The Mary Tyler Moore Show
The Six Million Dollar Man

AWARDS AND NOMINATIONS
Chiefs—Emmy Nomination
Ellis Island—Emmy Nomination
Shōgun—Emmy Award, DGA Award, Peabody Award

ACADEMY AWARD WINNERS
JERRY HAS WORKED WITH

Alan Arkin
Beatrice Straight
Bette Davis
Charlton Heston
Christopher Plummer
Cloris Leachman
Estelle Parsons
F. Murray Abraham
Faye Dunaway
Gregory Peck
Holly Hunter
Jack Palance
Joan Fontaine
Julie Christie
Karl Malden
Liza Minnelli
Patty Duke
Rita Moreno
Shirley Jones
Sir John Gielgud
Sissy Spacek
Timothy Hutton
Whoopi Goldberg

Printed in Great Britain
by Amazon

61770277R00127